REACHING THE NATIONS

By Mike Frisby

Published by RELATIONAL MISSION

REACHING THE NATIONS

RECOMMENDATIONS FOR LOCAL CHURCH LEADERS

How to: identify, prepare and support
local church members to become cross-cultural servants
in God's mission to disciple the nations.

Copyright © 2017 Mike Frisby

First published 1997

The right of Mike Frisby to be identified as the author of this work has been asserted by him in accordance with the Copyright, Designs and Patents Act 1988

All rights reserved. No part of this publication may be reproduced or transmitted in any form or by any means, electronic or mechanical, including photocopy, recording, or any information storage and retrieval system, without permission in writing from the publisher.

Published by Relational Mission

Jubilee Family Centre, Norwich Road, Aylsham, Norfolk, NR11 6JG, UK

www.relationalmission.com

ISBN 978-0-9954-77865

Acknowledgements

Scripture quotations taken from the Holy Bible, New International Version Anglicised Copyright © 1979, 1984, 2011 Biblica
Used by permission of Hodder & Stoughton Ltd, an Hachette UK company
All rights reserved.
'NIV' is a registered trademark of Biblica UK trademark number 1448790.

A catalogue record of this book is available from the British Library

Cover Design by Daniel Goodman

Typeset in Adobe Garamond Pro

CONTENTS

INTRODUCTION		1
1	**NO WELL-WORN PATHS!**	6
2	**INTRODUCTION TO THE NOTES FOR LEADERS**	27
3	**PROFILING THE PERSONNEL**	30
4	**CLARIFYING THE CALL**	46
5	**RESEARCHING THE ROUTE**	61
6	**SENDING THE SERVERS**	75
7	**MAINTAINING THE MOMENTUM**	108
8	**DEBRIEFING QUESTIONNAIRE**	113
9	**RECOMMENDED READING**	120
10	**QUESTIONNAIRES**	137
TEN OBSERVATIONS ON SHORT-TERM, LONG-TERM AND SECULAR WORK		166

ACKNOWLEDGEMENTS

I am grateful for the many friends and practitioners in the wider mission community whose insight, and sharing of personal experience has contributed so much to the material in this book. Especially, to those in the Global Connections network that seeks to serve, equip and develop churches in their mission.

My thanks too to those in Relational Mission and our wider Newfrontiers family, who through the years have stepped out courageously into cross-cultural mission overseas. It has been a privilege to work with you, and to learn from your life experience. Hopefully, lessons learnt together will enable those who come after you to travel the same road better prepared, and more effectively equipped and supported by their local churches.

I am also indebted to the many friends in the church families where I have served throughout the years that have so generously encouraged, prayed and supported me as I have sought to play my small part in making God's fame and renown known among the nations. You know who you are, and I trust that God will reward you for your many kindnesses and genuine friendship.

Thanks, most importantly, to my wife Denise, whose unending sacrificial love, encouragement and support in the past, and which continues to today, enables me to engage in motivating and equipping others to reach the nations for Christ.

A special thanks also to my now grown-up children, Rebecca, Tim and Lydia. In your younger years you so often "shared" dad so he could travel extensively around the United Kingdom, and in and out of many countries serving God's people. Your sacrifice has not gone unnoticed, and it is wonderful to see how God is blessing your lives and your own families.

As with any book, it takes numbers of people to produce, and my final thanks therefore, to Phil Whittall, Poppy Balding and Daniel Goodman who all had a hand in bringing this book to print.

INTRODUCTION

MIKE BETTS
Leader of Relational Mission

As I write this it seems that many nations are increasingly turning in on themselves. Yet whichever way the political wind is blowing and regardless of which ideology seems to have the upper hand one thing that must not change is that as Christians we care about the whole earth and all that is in it.

Our concern for God's glory means that we have a love for all peoples, languages, tribes, tongues and cultures. The whole world was made for Jesus and by Jesus, and His family will be gathered from every tribe and tongue, and the truth is that as believers we are "one new man in Christ". A mature expression of God's church on the earth will surely show us a gloriously diverse church.

God promised to Abraham that every people group on earth would be blessed, and we are Abraham's spiritual descendants in Christ (Galatians 3:29). Jesus promised that the end would come after the gospel of the kingdom had been preached in every nation (Matthew 24:14). He then commanded us to go and make disciples of every nation (Matthew 28:19). The call to the nations is clear and we want to embrace it.

We also believe that we are all on a mission together rather than simply sending 'missionaries'. In a globalised world many nations and cities are multi-cultural with hundreds of nationalities living side by side. In other words, we are all called to mission; wherever we are, whatever we are doing, whatever our role.

We have a calling as an apostolic people to see God's kingdom extended and established through the church. Jesus made it clear that as the Father had sent Him into this world, so He sends us into this world with the anointing of the Holy Spirit (John 20:21). There are still many places where the gospel hasn't yet reached, where churches are yet to be established. So there is still a need and a call for people to commit themselves to another nation for the sake of the gospel. How they do that well is the purpose of this small book by my friend Mike Frisby.

As a result of migration or mission more and more churches are now involved in cross-cultural work. We will need men and women to develop cross-cultural skills to enable them to fulfil that calling.

I am conscious that the needs of our day show us the urgency of being an apostolic people. This, of course, means that we are sent on mission. It also means that we have a clear understanding of apostolic ministry and authority as applying today. I am convinced that an apostolic and prophetic foundation must be laid in every church in every culture.

The scale of the task is still vast and we want to be co-operative with others in this great task. We also need to learn from others who have experience in areas of cross-cultural mission that we do not yet have. At the same time we should not hold back from emphasizing those things God has given us in our mission together.

It is vital that churches are founded on grace, not legalism. The ministries we read of in Ephesians 4 are still necessary for equipping the church. We love and long for the powerful combination of both Word and Spirit in the local church. The local church is to be the agent of the extension of the kingdom. The kingdom priorities of bringing good news to the poor, feeding the hungry, bringing justice and setting people free from oppression are essential for biblical church life.

We recognise that the outward expansion of the church in the book of Acts was sometimes spontaneous – as the Holy Spirit moved there was a scattering of the church in Jerusalem as they fled from persecution. At other times it was apostolic strategy prompted by the Holy Spirit in sending Barnabas and Saul to new churches like Antioch to help establish a right foundation. Both were moves of God and both required apostolic input either to establish or to confirm what had already been taking place.

We believe that the same will happen for us today. There will be those prompted by the Holy Spirit to move and be 'scattered' for whatever reason. As they go, they share their faith and then call on apostolic help lay good foundations in those churches. At other times there will be a clear strategy and investment involving those with recognised apostolic ministry.

INTRODUCTION

It is my prayer that there will be men and women in every church whom God has called to either join an existing team or to lead a new pioneering team to a city, nation or people group.

Mike Frisby has not just years of experience in this area but wisdom and gifting to help people make that journey from one culture to another. This small book will be an invaluable tool for every person and church wanting to work out their call to the nations. There are many suggestions on how this is worked out which enables people to become equipped towards the fulfilment of a call to other cultures.

We believe in working in teams rather than as individuals and we need people with different skills to make these teams strong and robust. It is never too early to start on this track if you feel you have such a call.

The world needs re-evangelising; there are vast areas with very few churches with the Gospel in the centre and holding Word & Spirit together. We need to play our part in this work. All this means there is a great need to equip our people well for cross-cultural mission and I commend this book to you for that purpose.

1
NO WELL-WORN PATHS!

In the nineteenth century friends of Dr David Livingstone, Scotland's most famous missionary and explorer wrote him the following message while he was serving in Africa: "We would like to send other men to you. Have you found a good road into your area yet?" Livingstone replied, "If you have men who will only come if there is a good road, I don't want them. I want men who will come if there is no road at all."

These challenging and stirring words of David Livingstone provide a much needed provocation to us in this the twenty-first century. They are also a reminder of a prophetic word given in a leaders' gathering back in the very early days of the Newfrontiers family of churches:

John Groves saw a herd of elephants running together towards a jungle. The way ahead looked totally impenetrable, but the elephants kept running forward and burst through the undergrowth, making a way where there was no way. Their combined strength broke through and a path was formed that others could subsequently use. The opening words of his prophecy were, "There are no well-worn paths ahead of you," and it continued, "Together you can accomplish more than you could ever accomplish alone."

Today we are looking for people to "make a way where there is no way". Ordinary people, who possess a similar kind of pioneer spirit to that which David Livingstone was looking for; men and women who, despite the cost, are willing to work sacrificially alongside others to see the kingdom of God extended throughout the whole earth.

In many parts of the world today people are waiting to hear the good news of salvation in Jesus for the very first time. Indeed, in order for some people groups to hear the gospel a literal road will need to be cut where no path currently exists!

For some people, serving God's purposes will involve them in crossing frontiers of a different kind – it will mean crossing new linguistic, social or cultural frontiers. For others it will be the opening up of new areas by the application of scientific and technological discoveries that accelerate and extend the advance of the gospel worldwide.

Each new generation faces not only a set of new challenges, but also an abundance of fresh God-given opportunities! Let me outline a few of the current challenges, not simply to inform, but hopefully to stir your faith as a local church to become involved in God's great plan to bless all the nations!

Let's start by looking at the term 'globalisation'. Definitions abound for this term, but it is generally agreed that globalisation is primarily about increasing economic integration.

In the developing or two-thirds world a good number of the population are so poor that they have very little to integrate and are often bypassed by new technologies, leading many commentators to suggest that globalisation is leading to a clear case of the rich getting richer while the poor get poorer!

Jimmy Carter, the former US President, called the growing disparity between rich and poor the "ultimate challenge of the twenty-first century". He remarked that, "there is an insensitivity even an unawareness in the rich developed world about the plight of people in the poverty stricken, underdeveloped world. It is a chasm that's growing and I don't see any encouraging movements in the US or Europe or Japan or other rich countries to address it".

The Bible witnesses to a God who works on behalf of the weak, the vulnerable, and the poor. He is depicted as being concerned about issues of justice, which must include global economic justice.

Scripture clearly states that part of our apostolic mission is to "remember the poor", something the Apostle Paul was eager to do! (Galatians 2:10)

It should not surprise us then that God expects us, as His people, to demonstrate a real concern for those whose social and economic standing expose them to exploitation and oppression. Our Christian witness must involve both social and political action on behalf of the poor.

Pope Francis recently wrote, in a paper on the proclamation of the gospel in today's world, "Each individual Christian and every community is called to be an instrument of God for the liberation and promotion of the poor, and for enabling them to be fully a part of society. This demands that we be docile (teachable) and attentive to the cry of the poor and come to their aid."

In today's world over a billion people lack access to clean water, while further billions lack adequate sanitation. Add to this the increase in natural disasters and it is not too difficult to understand World Vision's claim that "Every three seconds a child dies as a direct result of poverty."

One of the ways we could help meet the needs of some of the poorest peoples of the world would be by the provision of job-creation schemes or by encouraging sustainable small-scale enterprises run by the poor. However, if the workforce in developing countries is to take full advantage of these economic opportunities, attention must be given to both their education and health. Poverty has many faces. For some it centres on a lack of 'essentials' like food, clean water, adequate housing, health care, employment, schools and good roads. For others its focus is a lack of education, knowledge, skills or access to new technologies. For still others the crux of their poverty may lie in their inability to have any meaningful influence over their current well-being or future life.

Disaster response and relief, community and enterprise development, and advocacy are all ways the church can respond to the needs of the poor. However, the challenge is to respond in such a way that the poor are not demeaned or devalued. Any solution must involve working together with them; empowering them to create their own solutions and enabling them to make choices about their own future.

Responding to the needs of the world's poor opens wide a door of opportunity for people in our churches – business personnel, economists, lawyers, politicians, health workers, educationalists and many, many, others.

According to Jesus the gospel is first and foremost good news for the poor! What a privilege then that the local church, through the sharing of the gospel, can see men's and women's lives transformed by being restored to a right relationship with God and their fellow man.

James said to the early church, "Has not God chosen those who are poor in the eyes of the world to be rich in faith and to inherit the kingdom he promised those who love him?" (James 2:5)

Another feature of life in the twenty-first century is the growing urbanisation of our planet. Vast numbers of people are moving from the countryside into towns and cities. This movement is not only due to population growth and the search for adequate resources, but also people moving in search of a 'better' life.

A hundred years ago, two in ten people lived in cities. By 2010 around 50% of the world was urbanised, and currently the urbanised population is growing by 60 million per year. It is estimated that by the year 2030, six in ten people will be living in cities. (N.B. Growth in urbanisation in the less economically developed nations of the world doubled in the last half of the twentieth Century, particularly in Africa, Asia & South America.)

The economic and social problems that arise from urbanisation are well known. Pictures of the 'shanty towns' that often spring up in or around large cities in the developing world regularly hit our media, as do documentaries on the 'problems of the inner city'. Overcrowding, pollution, lack of housing and employment, crime, drugs, prostitution, vandalism, truancy, family and community breakdown, all combine to underline the fact that urban living in today's world is no easy option!

But, it is not all 'doom and gloom'! In many urban communities you can find great resilience, courage, local pride and profound human loyalty. Nevertheless, these areas need people who will sow hope, break down barriers and work alongside others to resolve local concerns and conflicts. We need followers of Jesus prepared to walk in His footsteps and "pitch their tent among them" in order to show urban dwellers what God is like. (See John 1:14).

Staying with the theme of people on the move, another of the key challenges that faces us today is that of migration.

The nineteenth century witnessed a move of people from their own shores out to other countries and continents. This was particularly true of people who went from Europe out to the great continents of Africa, Asia and South America. However, the twentieth century saw a movement in the opposite direction with many people from these great Continents returning to the 'motherland' or 'home' nation. At the start of the twenty-first century the movement of people both within and across national borders continues unabated.

Some move to escape natural disasters like floods or famine, while others move for economic reasons, to escape poverty or simply to better themselves. Many more move as the result of conflict and war and the ugly resurgence of 'ethnic cleansing'. Moving for the purposes of employment or education is not unusual in today's world.

The United Nations High Commissioner for Refugees (UNHCR) deals with asylum seekers, refugees returning home and displaced people within their own country. In 2016 their records showed 65.6 million forcibly displaced people of which, 40.3 million were internally displaced, 22.5 million were refugees and 2.8 million were asylum seekers.

Many nations today are dealing with the problems of oppression and violence towards ethnic minorities and immigrant communities. Facilitating integration and maintaining stability where people are acutely aware of those who 'have' and those who 'have not' is no easy task.

Yet, here again is an opportunity for the church to become involved. The church can act as an agent of reconciliation and change within its local community and can seek to influence key policy makers. Practical demonstrations of love and care can build important bridges into communities so that the gospel can be shared across cultures.

The nations are no longer 'over there' but right on our doorstep. Opportunities for churches abound among refugees and asylum seekers, to say nothing of the many thousands of international students, tourists and business people that visit our shores each year.

Talking of "right on our doorstep", here in the United Kingdom we must not forget the enormous needs of Europe, of which we are a part. Western Europe in particular needs re-evangelising.

Over the last hundred years or so secularism has swept through Western Europe. Many people have moved away from the certainties of Europe's Judeo-Christian heritage and many governments are dispensing with the very standards that once under-girded Europe's culture and development.

For many, God is considered to be dead or, at the very least, totally irrelevant. Christians are increasingly seen as a hindrance to social change and progress, and where the church does exist it is often considered to be a remnant of a bygone age.

Europe is seeing a breakdown in the family and the fragmentation of society. Feelings of isolation, loneliness and alienation abound and a once strong sense of community spirit is fading fast. Nevertheless, many people who are disillusioned with life are searching for a new spirituality. Some, as in the past, have turned to the occult, others to New Age thinking, new atheism, and numbers to eastern religious worldviews.

What an opportunity confronts us to show the relevance of Christ to these 'seekers' with their multiplicity of questions and personal struggles! We need hundreds of local churches who, by incarnation (living the truth) and by proclamation (telling the truth), demonstrate what it means to follow and live under the rule of King Jesus; vibrant communities full of the life of God, who act as salt and light and make known the manifold wisdom of God!

Another area of challenge is Europe's children, indeed the children of the whole world. What are the future prospects for the coming generations?

At this present time millions of children are involved in child labour, many in the most appalling conditions imaginable. Countless others live on the world's streets, and millions more are involved in the sex trade.

Over the last decade many children have been forced to become child soldiers and the ravages of war have seen millions left homeless, psychologically traumatised and physically disabled. It will take much time before these mental, physical and emotional scars are healed.

Children also suffer alongside their parents as a result of famine and natural disasters but are often much more vulnerable to sickness and disease. On many continents children are carrying the HIV virus and have witnessed the death of parents and relatives.

It is a scandal that, on average, more than 25,000 children under the age of five die each day from malnutrition and easily preventable diseases. Hiroshi Nakajima, The Director General of the World Health Organisation (WHO) called this "the silent genocide on our planet".

Over half of the world's population is now under 25 years of age, a third under 15 years of age. Of those under 15 years of age most live in the developing or two-thirds world and are often subject to many of the hardships and traumas we have just outlined.

As well as engaging in social and political action on behalf of the children and young people of the world we must also raise up key workers to specifically minister to the spiritual needs of the young.

Many believe there is evidence to show that large numbers of people take their first steps in following Christ between the ages of four and fourteen. Whether or not this view can be substantiated, there is no doubting that today among the young of the world, "the harvest is indeed plentiful but the labourers are few"!

One of the most important influences on the life of a child is its mother and in many countries women are the key agents of any social change. Some would say women are the key to reaching many of the world's resistant people groups with the gospel.

According to the World Health Organisation (WHO), the majority of the world's poor are women. Many of them suffer from inadequate or in some cases non-existent health care, with over half a million dying unnecessarily each year from pregnancy related complications. The AIDS pandemic has also resulted in many millions living with HIV infection and in more than a million dying each year from AIDS.

But it is not only in the area of health that women suffer. In key areas such as education, literacy, skills, employment, mobility and political representation women are constantly fighting an uphill battle. For example, the female workforce in the world is paid less than men for comparable work. There are also twice as many women as men among the world's illiterate people.

In recent years the introduction of community health projects, literacy and skills programmes has begun to improve the lot of many women around the globe. While this is to be applauded, nevertheless we must not deny the fact that there is still an enormous mountain to climb.

The Bible teaches the worth, dignity and equality of women in the sight of God, but this needs to be fleshed out and demonstrated before a watching world. We need vibrant Christian communities where women are fully participating and taking their rightful place in both the church and society. Local churches where husbands and wives exhibit the respect, honour and self-sacrifice taught in scripture and where practical love and concern flows constantly to widows and others in distress. (James 1:27)

Another of the great challenges facing us today, as in every generation, is the challenge of how to communicate the gospel.

Wycliffe Bible Translators (WBT) has demonstrated that the gospel accelerates among a people group once that people group have the Scriptures in their own 'heart' language. The Scriptures are vital in church planting for effective discipling of people, teaching, worship and leadership training.

New technologies are speeding up the translation process and WBT have a vision that by 2025, in partnership with others, they will have begun a translation project for every people group in the world that still needs one (approximately 2000).

Wrestling with linguistic and theological problems in translation is a major part of the current challenge, as is the production and distribution of the Scriptures once translation is complete. There is also the very real challenge where the language has never been written down before of teaching people how to read their very own new written language!

This may be considered a somewhat 'specialist' field but some in our churches may have the necessary aptitude for this work. The Scriptures are vital to on-going church planting work and we should encourage churches to co-operate with WBT and others in this field.

We must also remember that a great proportion of the world (estimated by some to be 26% of the world's population) is still illiterate. For example, nearly one out of every two people in the Middle East and two out of every three people in North Africa are illiterate. Yet in these regions nearly two-thirds of all households have access to modern media and technologies.

This raises the question of how we are to present the gospel to those who are illiterate, oral learners and those whose lives are being increasingly shaped by modern audio and visual technologies.

In recent years there has been an increasing engagement of Christians in the world of broadcasting either through the setting up of their own radio and television stations, through internet streaming or by acting as salt and light in the world's 'secular' media. Writers, producers, directors, actors, set designers, engineers and camera men can all play a part in the great commission.

There is no doubt that the medium of music is today's universal language, particularly among the younger generation. What we sometimes do not realise is that music is a way of penetrating and influencing a whole culture. Ethnomusicologists are increasingly being trained to work alongside church planting teams around the world. (N.B. Ethnomusicology is the study of music in its cultural context. Ethnomusicologists approach music as a social process in order to understand not only what music is but why it is: what music means to its practitioners and audiences, and how those meanings are conveyed.)

The modern communication technology revolution continues apace, with the number of users multiplying daily. (N.B. Such use is no longer restricted to the rich West!) While the secular commentators have seen these new technologies as developments of far greater significance than the invention of the printing press, most Christians still fail to see or harness their full potential for the gospel.

Christians that are using these technologies to dialogue with those of other faiths and to build relationships with people seeking to understand the Christian message suggest that there is room for yet further expansion and interaction from the churches via this medium.

This is not the place to debate the merits or otherwise of the use of modern media in the proclamation of the gospel, but it is worth flagging up that such a question does demand to be given careful thought and prayerful consideration. Especially so, when we consider that the rising generation of young people around the world almost exclusively learn by means of audio-visual technologies!

Whether or not we are prepared to enter this debate, it does illustrate another of the great challenges that faces every generation of believers, that is, the contextualisation of the gospel.

Contextualisation primarily has to do with how we translate, interpret and apply the Bible in our day and generation. It is about how we go about our evangelism, how we plant churches, how we demonstrate an 'incarnational' lifestyle, and the way we instruct people to live out their Christian commitment before a watching world.

But how do we communicate meaningfully to people whose culture knows nothing of the Bible or Jesus Christ? What about those whose worldview is governed by rational thinking or who have a materialistic mindset? How can we communicate the gospel meaningfully to a new generation that has lost faith in 'absolutes' and replaced them with the view that "What matters is what is true for you". A new generation that rejects the one 'big story' in favour of many stories, none of which are universally true.

What elements in individual cultures can be legitimately harnessed to assist a relevant and persuasive communication of the gospel? How can we help new believers work out their faith in everyday life without imposing on them our own cultural patterns of church life? Indeed, how can we ensure that the expression of Christianity among any people group remains true to Scripture yet relevant to modern life in the twenty-first century?

As in previous generations, these, and many similar questions demand both a thoughtful and prayerful response.

The challenge for all of us is to continue humbly seeking the mind of the Holy Spirit for God's wisdom and strategy to enable us to make disciples of all nations. Keeping in step with the Spirit is still the priority of today and every day!

We are convinced the Holy Spirit is underlining in our day and generation that it is time for the church of Jesus Christ to mobilise because the harvest is plentiful. "LET'S GO!" is more than a slogan, for it reverberates with the heartbeat of heaven.

Jesus' words to His disciples in Matthew 9:37-38 still hold relevance and significance today, "The harvest is plentiful but the workers are few. Ask the Lord of the harvest, therefore, to send out workers into His harvest field."

It is to the important task of mobilisation that we now turn.

As a worldwide family of apostolic teams together on a mission to establish the kingdom of God we are looking for people who despite the inconvenience, stress and hardships involved are prepared to play their part in discipling the nations. Those who like the martyred American missionary Jim Elliott can truly say "He is no fool who gives what he cannot keep to gain what he cannot lose."

People who have counted the cost and are willing to use their God-given gifts, talents and skills to advance God's kingdom in the world. Some will be needed to join existing teams, but increasing numbers will be needed for pioneer teamwork amongst many of the unreached peoples of the world. Whether their involvement is six days, six months or six years, their contribution could prove invaluable to the advance of God's kingdom.

But where are these people? How do we identify them? Having identified them how do we train and prepare them to go? When they have gone how do we support them? What happens when they return home again? These are some of the natural questions that arise for any local church leadership and the rest of this book is an attempt to both answer these types of questions and to equip you practically to serve your people and the purposes of God in our generation.

2
INTRODUCTION TO THE NOTES FOR LEADERS

An increasing number of people within our churches are sensing the call of God to become involved in cross-cultural ministry to reach the nations for Christ. But is their call genuine? If it is genuine, then how do we help them prepare to face the realities of cross-cultural mission in today's world? How does a local church practically equip and release increasing numbers of people into the harvest to accomplish God's purpose "to bring all things in heaven and on earth together under one head, even Christ"? (Ephesians 1:10)

The following notes have been written to help you as church leaders to explore with people the genuineness of their call and to begin to help them take the necessary steps that will lead them to serve God in a different culture from their own. You will also find a section on how you can support people when the decision has finally been made to send them overseas.

As you work through the notes you may like to write down the answers to the questions. Doing so will help you to focus your thinking and reflect on the suitability of the person for cross-cultural ministry. If you don't know some of the answers, then obtain the necessary information from someone else in the church that does.

The notes can be used as a tool for exploring some of the crucial issues surrounding serving in a cross-cultural situation. However, at the end of this book you will also find a series of questionnaires based on these leadership notes, for completion by those wanting to serve cross-culturally. The completed questionnaires can form the basis for face-to-face interviews/discussions with your people. (N.B. As an alternative you could decide not to have the questionnaires completed, but simply to select some specific questions from the individual questionnaires in order to form your own list of topics for discussion.)

Although not comprehensive, we trust that these leadership notes will go a long way in helping you serve those offering themselves for cross-cultural ministry. If you require clarification on any point or further help, then please do not hesitate to get in touch with the author (If he doesn't know the answer, he probably knows someone else who does!).

A recommended reading list of books on issues surrounding cross-cultural mission is given at the back of this book. We hope the books listed will stimulate your own thinking and provide you with a greater understanding of cross-cultural mission. They should also prove a useful resource to both you and your people as together you work through the equipping and sending process.

Finally, before you embark on working through the leadership notes may I take this opportunity to remind you that sending out people and giving them adequate support is both a great privilege and responsibility for the local church. It involves both time and commitment not only by the leadership team but also by the whole church. It should therefore be approached prayerfully, looking for the grace of God to enable you to serve faithfully those among you that are called to be cross-cultural servants in the task of world evangelisation.

3
PROFILING THE PERSONNEL

While the old saying still holds true that "availability is more important than ability" and Scripture teaches that "the Lord chooses the weak to confound the strong", nevertheless, there are some basic qualities one is looking for in those offering themselves for cross-cultural work. (See Judges 6:11-16, 1 Samuel 16:1-13, 1 Corinthians 1:26-31)

Good training can develop character and skills, and good teaching can rectify a lack of knowledge. However, serious flaws in any area will not disappear simply because the person is transported into a new and exciting environment! As a general rule of thumb, if you would not be happy giving responsibility to them and using their gifts in your own local church, then they are not ready for cross-cultural work at home or in other nations.

The following sections will stimulate you to think realistically about the person wishing to serve cross-culturally. Remember, we are not looking for perfection, but neither do we want to pass over deficiencies that stare us in the face! Shortcomings do not have to mean disqualification, but rather provide us with the opportunity to help a person to develop and grow by good discipling and training.

CHARACTER

Many of these character traits reflect the list of qualities set out for church elders. (See 1 Timothy 3:1-7)

CREDITABLE

- Do they demonstrate a consistent Christian lifestyle?
- Is there evidence of change and growth taking place?
- Do others in the church speak well of them?
- Do outsiders speak well of them?
- What does their employer or work colleagues think about them?

- Have you any doubts about their moral integrity?

Dependable

- Would you describe them as reliable, hardworking, and always ready to see a job through to the end?
- Do they show responsibility in handling their financial affairs?
- Have you any evidence that they continue to function well during periods of pressure?
- Do they cope well with frustration, stress or failure?
- Do they balance their time well in order to fulfil their work, family and church commitments?
- Are there any signs of a lack of self-control or self-discipline?

Teachable

- Do they exhibit a humble, teachable spirit and readiness to learn? (See Isaiah 66:2)
- Is there ample evidence that they are not dogmatic in their views and that they are open to correction? (See Proverbs 9:8, Proverbs 19:25)

- Have they shown signs of being able to adapt or remain flexible in the face of changing circumstances? (See Philippians 4:11,12)

GENEROUS

- Would you describe them as considerate, generous and open-handed? (See Matthew 5:43-48)
- Do they exhibit an unselfish attitude and a desire to serve others?
- Have they shown an interest in and/or a willingness to work alongside the wider body of Christ?

NATURAL

- Would you describe them as balanced and well-adjusted people?
- Is there evidence that they accept themselves for who they are?
- Do they exhibit a common sense approach to life?
- Are they able to laugh at themselves?
- Do they demonstrate that they enjoy life rather than merely endure it?

Fruitful

- Is the fruit of the Holy Spirit seen in their life? (See Galatians 5:22-23)
- Do they exhibit both a patient and a forgiving spirit?
- Is their faith evidenced by a pattern of good works and acts of kindness? (See Galatians 5:6, Ephesians 2:10, Titus 2:14, James 2:14-17)

Resourceful

- Do they exhibit strength of character without being angular or individualistic?
- Have they shown any signs of an adventurous and courageous spirit?
- Are they willing to tackle new initiatives?
- Would you describe them as people able to take their own initiative, yet remaining interdependent?

RELATIONAL SKILLS

One of the most important qualities we are looking for in someone working cross-culturally is their ability to get on with a wide range of people. As people will work in a team setting they will need to develop the necessary skills to handle any relational conflict that may arise through differences of personality and opinion.

RELATING TO OTHERS

How do you rate their ability to relate to the following types of people?

- Same sex
- Opposite sex
- Children
- Senior citizens
- Peer group
- The sick and disabled
- The wider Body of Christ.

SUBJECT TO AUTHORITY

- Is there evidence of them showing honour and respect for those "over them in the Lord"? (See 1 Thessalonians 5:12-13; Hebrews 13:17)

- Would you describe them as submissive and willing to be held accountable for their actions rather than argumentative and independent?
- Is there evidence that in a team situation they are fully able to receive direction and accept correction from others?

TOLERANCE

- Have they shown any ability to get on with others who are markedly different from them either in personality, social background or academic ability?
- Does their enthusiasm for working with people from other cultures stem from real life encounters or past experience working with another ethnic group?

CONFLICT

- Would you describe them as a peacemaker – ready to make every effort to maintain harmony within the Body of Christ? (See Romans 12:18; Ephesians 4:3)

- Do they resolve conflicts quickly in a biblical manner or do they tend to harbour grudges over an extended period? (See Matthew 18:15-17)
- Have they exhibited a truly forgiving spirit when they have been wronged? (See Matthew 18:21-35; Ephesians 4:31-32; Colossians 3:13)

SELF-GIVING

- Would you describe their personality as cohesive, in that they are able to both give and receive affection?
- Have they demonstrated an ability to empathise with others and provide encouragement and support to those going through difficult times? (See 2 Corinthians 1:3-4)
- In working with others, do they show genuine friendship and interest in the well-being of others in the group or do they simply relate on a functional level? (See Philippians 2:3-4; 1 Thessalonians 2:8)
- Are they genuinely pleased when others receive blessing or recognition not afforded to them? (See Romans 12:10)

FAMILY

It is vital that the whole family is united about any move into cross-cultural work. Consideration must also be given to the practical and emotional effects that any such move may have on the extended family, particularly any unsaved relatives.

At the end of the day people must obey God rather than be deflected from their call by any adverse reactions from "well-meaning" relatives or friends. However, thought must be given to the fulfilment of the biblical injunction to care for those of our own family. (See 1 Timothy 5:8)

SINGLE

- Have they thought about the effect serving cross-culturally might have on their current friendships?
- Have they considered the full impact their current decision may make on any desire to marry in the future?
- Is there a current romantic attachment that needs resolving in the light of their future intention to serve in other nations?

- Has the subject of serving in other nations been discussed with their parents and if so what was their reaction?
- Do they have any on-going commitments or responsibilities towards their relatives, and if so how do they see these being worked out in the future?

MARRIED

- Are you sure that both husband and wife are united in their proposal to serve cross-culturally?
- Would you describe the marriage as happy and stable?
- Are you reasonably certain that there are no major unresolved issues in the marriage?
- Are you confident that the couple are open and good communicators between themselves?
- Do they relate well to other couples in the church?
- Does the couple have a proven track record of coming through particular periods of pressure and difficulty in their married life?

- If the couple are currently without children, have they thought through the implications of having and rearing children in a different culture?

(N.B. The same questions should be asked regarding parents and relatives as in the section above headed 'Single'.)

CHILDREN

- As far as you are aware are the children happy and well adjusted?
- In what respects do the children reflect their parents' character?
- Are you sure that, where applicable, their children have been able to express their views on the possibilities of the family serving in a cross-cultural situation?
- Have the parents thought through the implications and options for the future education of their children?

HEALTH

Good physical health is a great advantage but poor health is not necessarily a bar to cross-cultural service in other nations.

It may simply restrict the number of options available in which a person may serve.

- How would they describe their general health?
- How frequently have they seen their own GP in the last year?
- Are there any current health problems that they or their family are experiencing?
- Do they (or their children) have any physical handicaps?
- Have they (or any near relative) ever suffered from or received treatment/counselling for emotional or mental illness?
- Does your personal knowledge of them lead you to believe that they are emotionally and mentally stable?
- Have they ever had to leave a job or had a job contract terminated because of an inability to cope?
- Do you know of any traumatic past experience that is still affecting their attitudes and behaviour today?

(For example: abuse, bereavement, failure, rejection, major accident, etc.)

QUALIFICATIONS & WORK EXPERIENCE

There are many more nations open to the Christian cross-cultural worker than people imagine, but increasingly the possession of some kind of professional qualification or skill will open the door more readily into the country of service.

SECULAR

- What academic or professional qualifications does the person possess?
- Are they currently studying or proposing to study for a recognised professional qualification?
- In what areas do they consider they have obtained a good degree of competency even though they have no professional qualification?
- Does their past employment record reveal any skills or abilities that could be useful in another country?

- Are they the kind of person that would be willing to train or re-train to obtain a qualification that would allow them entry into another country?
- How would you assess their willingness and ability to learn new skills and to cope with a training programme?

CHURCH

- What kind of formal or informal training have they received in biblical, theological and pastoral issues?
- Have they been trained in or equipped in any specialist areas of ministry? (For example: children's work, healing, deliverance, abuse counselling, etc.)
- What specific training/equipping experiences do they consider have prepared them for the task of being a cross-cultural worker in another nation?
- Can they describe the particular areas of church life where they feel they are competent to minister and have been fruitful?
- Are you able to concur with their own assessment of their ministry?

- Has their experience of church life been limited to one local church or do they have experience of working in a number of different churches/congregations

LIFE SKILLS

Those serving cross-culturally in other nations will encounter both sophisticated and primitive environments, advanced technologies and outdated structures. In order to survive they will need to have or to develop a number of life skills. While acknowledging that even day to day living can become a much more complex affair in a new culture, nevertheless it is helpful to try and make an initial assessment of some of the skills already possessed by those indicating a desire to serve cross-culturally in other nations.

- Do you consider them competent to manage the basic areas of everyday living? (For example: cooking, hygiene, budgeting etc.)

- Do they possess any basic DIY-type skills? (For example: painting, decorating, plumbing, carpentry etc.)
- Do they have any basic engineering/mechanical skills? (For example: electrics, car maintenance etc.)
- Do they have some basic knowledge of first aid, health issues or nursing skills?
- Are they happy with modern technologies and could they be described as computer literate?
- Are there any other specific skills they possess which they think may be of benefit in a cross-cultural setting? (For example: research skills)
- Have they shown any aptitude or ability for learning foreign languages?

4
CLARIFYING THE CALL

If we were honest most of us would like a definite unmistakable call to serve God, attended with supernatural signs. After all, wasn't this the way it was for God's servants in the past? (For example: Moses at the burning bush; Isaiah in the Temple; Saul on the Damascus road.)

Today, we still hear stories of similar dramatic encounters with God that set the course of a person's life and ministry. However, the plain truth is that for most people their call to serve cross- culturally will be an on-going process over a period of time that builds to an utter certainty of the will of God for their lives. The important thing to remember is that God knows people individually and will lovingly guide him or her into the unique part He has planned for them to play in the extension of His kingdom on the earth.

On some occasions in the past people were sent to other nations who were not seemingly "well prepared and ready to go". Nevertheless, those who proved in the end to be wonderfully effective in their cross-cultural ministry give testimony to the fact that it was a clear call to cross-cultural work in another nation that strengthened and sustained them through many difficult times.

So what are some of the common elements in this vital area of a person's call to cross-cultural work in another nation? The following notes are designed to help you work through with people their own sense of call to establish whether or not it is a genuine call of God to cross-cultural work in another nation.

MOTIVATION

Are you convinced that the desire to serve cross-culturally springs from divine constraint rather than a simple recognition of need? (See 2 Corinthians 5:14)

The following are a list of wrong motives:

- Desire for status or recognition.

- Desire for a change of scene because of discontent with their current situation.
- Seeking to escape from unhappy domestic, work or church situations.
- A feeling of superiority that concludes that the "privileged" must serve the "deprived".
- Guilt because of comparative cultural affluence or perception that their current ministry is spiritually inept.
- Itchy feet – a desire to travel and experience new cultures or simply enjoy new experiences.
- Romanticism – feeling they will be more fulfilled as people or that other cultures are less corrupt.

REALISM

The Lord Jesus taught the importance of counting the cost of discipleship before we follow Him. (See Luke 14:25-35)

- Do they have a realistic view of working cross-culturally in regard to the possible loneliness, difficulties and sacrifice it could entail? (For example: future career, material wealth, pension provision, etc.)

- Have they sufficient detailed knowledge of their proposed sphere of service to form a sound judgement about their possible involvement? (For example: skills needed, language requirements, job description, knowledge of target people group or nation etc.)
- Have they had the opportunity to talk with anyone who is currently working (or has previously worked) in the same or similar sphere of service to the one in which they want to engage?
- Are they able to articulate their personal strengths and weaknesses and any pressure points that they think may arise in their future ministry?

SPIRITUAL MATURITY

We wish to underline again that the Lord often chooses and uses inadequate and weak people (See 1 Corinthians 1:26-31). We are not to look for "perfection", but we are to look for those who show clear evidence of the following characteristics in their lives:

- A personal, intimate and growing relationship with God
- A devotion to prayer
- An ability to feed themselves from the Scriptures
- A dependence on the power and presence of the Holy Spirit
- A godly lifestyle evidencing the fruit of the Holy Spirit
- A life of grace rather than legalism
- A genuine love for the body of Christ
- A living faith that has stood the test of trials
- A concern for the lost and a desire to see them saved

- An openness to fresh revelation from God and a determination to press on to maturity in Christ

EFFECTIVE MINISTRY

When the Holy Spirit called for Saul and Barnabas to be set aside for the work of reaching the nations they were already men who had an effective teaching and prophetic ministry (See Acts 13:1-3). Today, not every potential cross-cultural worker will have years of effective ministry behind him or her. However, it should be noted that if people do not function well while serving in their own local church environment, then they often do not function effectively in ministry when they move into a different culture.

Or to put it another way, "If abilities have not been mastered in one's 'home' territory, it is difficult to customize them to new circumstances. Lack of ministry experience in one's home culture is not a good indicator of success elsewhere." (David Pollock – *Doing Member Care Well, Perspectives and Practices from around the World* p.27)

In essence we are not looking for people with a 'cross-cultural' gifting but rather people who want to employ their 'existing' gifts (natural and spiritual) in a cross-cultural sphere. While training will be needed to help them apply their gifts in a sensitive and appropriate manner to their new culture, nevertheless their basic gifts will probably remain the same.

- What do you consider to be their basic natural and spiritual gifts at this moment in time?
- Have they shown skill and effectiveness in the ministry area in which they feel God is calling them to serve? (For example: evangelism, pastoring, preaching/teaching, youth work, social action, etc.)
- If the measure of their effectiveness is small, are they receiving or will they receive on-going discipleship/training?
- If they are entering a totally new field of work, do you believe that the necessary skills related to the new sphere of activity can be developed during the home preparation/training period?

(N.B. There is sometimes a tension between staying longer in the home nation in order to obtain new skills and leaving immediately after the normal preparation period. Each case needs to be treated on its merits, especially in light of the fact that it may be more expedient and relevant to obtain the new skills once in the new nation.)

- Is there good evidence of their ability to listen to others and to clearly articulate and communicate their own views?

Not all will be called to serve in a leadership capacity in another nation but if they are:

- How do you rate their ability in regard to management and/or leadership skills?
- Have they shown an ability to train and pass on skills to others, thus reproducing their ministry? (See 2 Timothy 2:1-2)

CALL OF GOD

The scriptures testify to the fact that 'the call of God' comes to people in many different ways. (See Genesis 12:1; Exodus 3:2; Isaiah 6:1; Amos 3:8; Acts 16:9)

Although there is a sense in which we all have a 'general' call to the nations, nevertheless it is vital that each person sensing a call to cross-cultural work in another nation should be able to articulate their own specific call from God.

At the start a person's call may be of a broader nature and indeed in some cases may be hard for people to put into words. The aim of this section is to help you in exploring 'the call' with each person so that they can be certain of what God is saying to them. The goal is to seek to move 'the call' out of the realm of the general and into the specific, in order to see them mobilised for cross-cultural work in another nation.

The following is a list of general categories of call experienced by individuals. How many of these broad classifications apply to the person you are dealing with?

- "I feel a wide sense of call to other cultures." (For example: Paul was called to the Gentiles)
- "I feel called to join another person in their cross-cultural work." (For example: Timothy joined Paul on his apostolic mission to reach the nations) (N.B. It is not unusual for people to want to give themselves to apostolic leadership without a specific nation in mind.)
- "'I feel called to a particular kind of people." (For example: the poor, business people, children, etc.)
- "I feel called to a specific country." (For example: India, Malawi, Ukraine, China, etc.)
- "I feel called to a specific people group." (For example: the Fulani, the Kurds, the Uzbeks, etc.)
- "I feel called to a particular value system." (For example: "The church planting vision and values of Newfrontiers have gripped my heart and I

would serve with this family of churches anywhere in the world.")
- "I feel called to a particular type of spiritual ministry." (For example: teaching, evangelism, pastoral work, etc.)
- "I feel called to use my professional/vocational skills." (For example: nursing, teaching, engineering, etc.)
- "I feel called to . . . . . ."

  (If none of the above fit try to discover what best describes their own situation)

Usually, there are two facets that combine to bring certainty about God's call:

The subjective: the inner conviction that comes through the voice and witness of the Holy Spirit and the objective: the outward confirmation that comes through a combination of some of the circumstances outlined below:

- Advice and counsel received from church leaders and trusted friends.

- God speaking through passages of Scripture.
- Prayers and prophecies that confirm what is already in their heart.
- Supernatural happenings – visions, dreams, angelic visitations, etc.
- Divine appointments – meeting key individuals who have a relevancy and impact as regards their proposed future sphere of service.
- Collaboration of circumstances – doors opening; being in the right place at the right time; needed job or finances being supplied; etc.
- Confirmation after action – God honouring steps of faith taken.
- Encouragement and prayerful support from other members of the church.

Which of the above specifically apply to the person?

Other questions you may need to ask:

- Is the person clear and sure about their call?

- Can you see a pattern of a consistent and repeated call in their life?
- Is the family unit united concerning this call?
- Does their spouse have an awareness of an individual call or do they simply feel caught up in this call because of their marriage? (N.B. Some spouses, while not sensing a direct call to a nation, feel called to serve their spouse's ministry or calling and are therefore happy and secure to go to a given nation.)

If there is any doubt over the leading of the Holy Spirit, remember God has promised to clearly guide all those who seek him with a trusting and humble heart. (See Psalm 25:9&12, Psalm 32:8, Psalm 48:14, Proverbs 3:5-6)

If there are serious concerns about the genuineness of the call it may be better to prayerfully seek God together for a period to obtain further clarity on the issue.

LOCAL CHURCH

It is clear from Scripture that when Saul and Barnabas were sent out they were commissioned from their home base and later returned to it to give account of God's gracious work that had been accomplished through them. (See Acts 13:1-3, Acts 14:26-28)

If you are convinced of God's call on your people's lives for cross-cultural work, then in fellowship with your apostolic team you will need to decide both the kind of support and the level of support you as a church are willing to give them and for how long?

- Are you convinced of both their suitability and availability for the task ahead?
- If you have doubts in any aspect of their suitability is this because of a genuine weakness/deficiency or does it emanate from the fact that their going may hinder your own longings and ambitions for your own local church?

- Have you considered the financial implications involved and reached a decision as to whether they will finance themselves through some kind of employment; raise their own support; be supported by the local church; a combination of some or all of these?
- Are you prepared to provide or support any necessary training needed during the period of preparation for work in another culture?
- Do you have enough people resources to give adequate support to them during the preparation time and when they leave to serve in another culture? (See the chapter on "Sending the Servers.")
- If it is decided to move forward on the proposal, is there a mechanism that will provide for good pastoral care and accountability?
- Can you from the heart say, "It seems good to the Holy Spirit and us"?

5
RESEARCHING THE ROUTE

This section is designed to help you begin to deal with the detailed outworking of a person's call to become a cross-cultural servant in the task of world evangelisation. It will help you move them from their point of intention, to actual involvement in a different culture or nation. A number of factors will need to be considered.

Most people will need further training of some sort, coupled with a period of preparation and orientation for their work in the new culture. How this is facilitated will depend both on the individual's personal circumstances and the complexities of the culture they will be entering. It cannot be emphasised too strongly that each person needs to be treated as an individual and that the training and preparation package be tailored to meet their specific requirements.

As early as possible, seek to contact your apostolic team so that they can be involved in the process of formulating a training and preparation package.

Before we look at some of the practical issues we need to mention that some church planting teams are joint ventures with mission agencies that have a particular expertise in a given country or region. Agreements with these agencies should be made to ensure both parties are clear on lines of authority, accountability and pastoral oversight. Should you therefore have a case where it appears there is a potential for a joint venture, then please contact the leadership of your apostolic team for further guidance.

You will need to give thought to some of the following practical issues:

LONG-TERM/SHORT-TERM

The benefits or otherwise of working long-term or short-term cross-culturally are shown on the table of observations at the end of this book. (This table also compares the advantages/disadvantages of working in secular employment in a cross-cultural setting in another nation.) You may like to use this table to help people clarify what is the best option for them personally or as a family.

It may also be helpful at this stage to begin discussing some of the possible financial repercussions of serving short- or long-term in another culture. For example, will it be necessary for them to make provision for a future pension? Will they need to provide financially for their children's future education? Will it be better to sell or rent out any existing property? How will they use or invest any regular income or surplus funds? (N.B. In many of these areas it may be necessary to seek some professional advice before coming to concrete decisions.)

Short-term service generally means a period of anything up to two years. Working short-term can not only make a significant contribution to God's work in the world but it is often the precursor to long-term involvement in another nation.

Generally speaking, if a person is going to work long-term in another culture they will need a longer and more thorough period of preparation and training.

SHORT-TERM OPPORTUNITIES

Being part of a short-term team in another nation is a great way for people to test their suitability for cross-cultural work and to grow as a person. Working with or alongside churches already involved in reaching out across cultures will enable people to gain valuable experience and insight into cross-cultural work.

As well as teams in other nations there are usually numerous opportunities to experience cross-cultural work in people's home countries. It may be as simple as spending time with a church that already works with students from overseas or is situated in an area where it is reaching out to various ethnic groups within their community.

BIBLICALLY GROUNDED

It is essential that all those involved in seeking to reach people from another culture be well grounded in the Scriptures. They should have a good grasp of the principles of interpretation of Scripture (hermeneutics) and proven ability in applying the Scriptures to their everyday lives. We are looking for self-feeders who love the word of God and are seeking to be obedient to its teaching. (See 2 Timothy 2:15)

The level of biblical competency required will depend largely on the sphere of future ministry activity. Has the person attained a sufficient level of biblical competency? Could they benefit from further training? Are there suitable training options within your own local church or region?

It can also be helpful to ascertain whether or not there are specific subjects or areas of doctrine or practice that are relevant to their intended sphere of service. (For example: justice, suffering, restitution, sovereignty of God, Spiritism, idolatry, family life, singleness, ancestors, angels, demons, etc.)

If there are specific issues, then all that may be necessary is a simple refresher course covering what the Bible says on the subject. However, on some issues you may need to seek out a specialist course or seminar for them to attend. You could also recommend books for them to read or provide your own study programme for them to follow.

Once they have grasped the truth they will need to learn how to communicate it cross-culturally, but we will deal with this area later in this book.

MINISTRY

Whenever possible, draw up or obtain a detailed job description for the particular ministry area in which they intend to serve. Note down the relevant skills required for them to function effectively in the area of ministry and compare this with their current skills, spiritual gifting and experience.

If the comparison shows a lack of a skill, an inadequate level of competency or deficiency of experience, discuss together how this can be rectified. Any shortfall will probably need to be addressed before people are sent out, but on some occasions can be rectified once people are resident in their country of service. (For example: further language study, greater cultural awareness, etc.)

It is essential to consult with the team or church to which they will be assigned to receive their agreement to take responsibility for any future training needs.

Training courses are designed to train people in the three areas of knowledge, character and skills. For full details of these courses contact your apostolic team.

SPECIALIST COURSES

From time to time you will have people that require specialist training of one form or another. This may be to enhance or equip them for their ministry or to provide a legitimate form of entry for them into a restricted access nation.

For example, the International Training Network based in Bournemouth, specialises in offering courses in Teaching English as a Foreign Language as a means of participating in world mission. Similarly, Youth With A Mission (YWAM) run a helpful course called, "An Introduction to Medical Missions", dealing with primary health care issues and a variety of clinical subjects.

It will be a question of finding the right course to suit your people but there are a number of outstanding courses available here in the UK and worldwide. You can use the following two websites to help you identify a particular course or alternatively contact someone in the leadership of your own apostolic team.

- Global Connections, the UK Evangelical Network for World Mission at: www.globalconnections.org.uk
- Oscar, the UK Information Centre for World Mission www.oscar.org.uk

(N.B. If you are outside the UK then you may wish to contact the equivalent body in your own nation)

CROSS-CULTURAL TRAINING TRACK

It is not easy to adapt to living in a different culture where people think and act in a way that is alien to all that we have known. To live in this new environment and particularly to communicate the good news of Jesus will entail both humility and the learning of new skills. People will need to learn to see the Bible through the eyes of the people of their new host culture and discover ways of communicating God's truth in words and actions that are appropriate and sensitive to their new cultural setting.

Various day, weekend and week-long training courses take place from time to time and details of these can be found by contacting your own apostolic team.

The training courses cover important subjects related to cross-cultural mission including knowing your call, communicating the gospel cross-culturally, relating to other faiths, and issues regarding language learning, to give a few examples.

The courses are designed in such a way as to help people progressively move from an initial sense of calling to taking the necessary steps of preparation for serving in another nation. This stepped approach means people move from a general introduction to cross-cultural mission and an exploration of their own sense of call to a more in-depth look at and preparation for church planting in another culture.

Self-study

In order to help people develop relevant skills they can also engage in some self-study. At the back of this manual you will find a recommended reading list. Among these are a number of good books and study guides that will specifically assist people's preparation for working in a different culture.

On the secular market there are also helpful materials that can broaden people's awareness of different cultures and the state of the nations. (For example: Travel Guides, National Geographic, New Internationalist, UNICEF – State of Nations Report, etc.)

RESIDENTIAL TRAINING

For some people wishing to serve in another culture on a long-term basis a period of extended and more in-depth residential training may be necessary. For example, when people have been in another nation for a period of time they may need to return home to train in more depth in some specific area of cross-cultural ministry related to their work.

If you feel this is the case, then this should be discussed with your apostolic team so that they can investigate and advise on any possible residential modules or courses that would help equip your people.

LIFE SKILLS

In addition to the life skills people already possess they may need to develop new ones. This will depend largely on the intended geographical location, and factors such as the social, economic and technological infrastructure of the country.

Others may need a 'refresher' course of some sort to bring them up to date or acquaint them with the specific peculiarities pertaining to a given country (For example: medical care/procedures).

On other occasions it may be necessary for people to upgrade or gain new professional qualifications. This may make access to their intended country of service easier, and themselves more effective in their receiving nation.

You will have to research the availability of courses to meet individual needs but a good example would be the Adult Education prospectus from the Local Education Authority in the UK. (N.B. The enormous range of subjects and skills available may surprise you!)

There is also a great opportunity for people with specific practical skills in your local church to become involved in world mission. They are a great resource and can be encouraged to pass on their 'expertise' and 'know how' by apprenticing those going to other nations.

We must not forget, either, the enormous resource of those who have already lived and worked in different areas of the world over many years. There is no substitute for experience and with a little thought one can usually find or track down someone who is willing to pass on their intimate knowledge of living in a specific location abroad.

LANGUAGE

Language learning tends to develop best when people are placed in an environment where they need to use that foreign language on a daily basis. Living among nationals is therefore of great value, but this is not often possible until people are actually living in another nation.

Formal language training is a great help, but not everyone is well suited to the classroom environment or particularly gifted with an aptitude for learning foreign languages. Wycliffe Bible Translators run helpful courses that give a foundation for language learning and it is well worth contacting them to discover what is currently on offer. (www.wycliffe.org.uk Email: askus@wycliffe.org Telephone: 01494 569100)

However, people can begin to learn a language before going or being involved in another culture and you may like to suggest to them one of the following options:

- Linguaphone course

It is still considered one of the best methods! (N.B. This is sometimes available at local libraries in the UK.)

- BBC course

This has the advantage that many courses include cultural information as well as straight language learning.

- Night school

Many Adult Education Centres offer courses for beginners and advanced classes. (N.B. An increasing number of courses are now available during the day.)

- Personal tutor

In our multi-national societies, foreign speakers often live alongside us and are willing to give tutoring for a small fee. (N.B. You can sometimes negotiate a good deal by offering to teach them English in return for them teaching you!)

Note: Because of the growing universal acceptance of the English language, it is possible today to get by in many nations of the world by speaking only English. Nevertheless, foreign nationals always appreciate the effort made on our part to learn their language. To speak in their mother tongue not only opens the way for good communication, but also opens the door for genuine friendship and their hearts to the gospel.

It is important to emphasise that language learning is a continual process – one that will never stop! Not only is it important for people to learn the 'words', but also the way of thinking – how ideas are developed, expressed and communicated.

6
SENDING THE SERVERS

In the Gulf War it took twenty support personnel to keep one soldier fighting on the battle field. Today, we need a similar army of support people behind those serving in cross-cultural contexts. We need people who understand the realities of spiritual warfare and the vital role that support plays in reaching the nations for Christ.

The apostle Paul in his letter to the Philippians constantly gives thanks to them for their "partnership in the gospel" (Philippians 1:3-4). Along with their love and prayers, they contributed financially time and time again to his mission. It is obvious that Paul valued their support and saw their help as an essential contribution to the advance of the gospel.

The support role provides us with an opportunity to catch up many people in our local church into the task of world evangelisation; encouraging them to use their own spiritual gifts and natural abilities to serve those sent out to other nations. This section aims to stimulate your thinking on six major areas of support, and suggests some practical steps that could be taken to serve those being sent out into a cross-cultural setting.(N.B. For a fuller treatment of the subject of local church support see the book *Serving as Senders* by Neal Pirolo from which some of the key points that follow were gleaned. Alternatively, for a shorter summary also based on the book see "Sender's guide" by Mike Frith on the Oscar or Stewardship websites: www.oscar.org.uk or www.stewardship.or.uk)

What follows is an attempt to encourage 'best practice'. There may well be occasions when not everything highlighted below is in place before you send someone to serve in another nation. Do continue to be flexible and obedient to the leading of the Holy Spirit, and at the same time serve and care for those sent to the best of your God-given ability.

MORAL SUPPORT

The Scriptures are strong on their emphasis of the need to encourage and build each other up. (For example: 1 Thessalonians 5:11, Hebrews 3:13, Hebrews 10:25)

Sadly, those feeling called to cross-cultural ministry often receive discouragement, rather than encouragement. When people declare their intentions to serve abroad, it is not uncommon to hear such comments as:

- "But you are needed here."
- "Who is going to pay?"
- "Don't you think it's a waste of your education?"
- "But you will be taking your children away from their grandparents."
- "Won't you lose the chance of marrying?"
- "What about your future career prospects?"

There is therefore a great need for people to provide constant positive encouragement and feedback to those contemplating going abroad. Indeed, moral support will be required throughout the whole process of preparation and sending, and is unlikely to diminish once people are actually living abroad!

Here are some suggested means of providing this support:

VERBAL AFFIRMATION

It is important for us to articulate our support of them. Simple statements like:

- "We are right behind you."
- "We are excited by your vision."
- "We want to know more about what God has laid on your heart."
- "We will miss you, but we want to help you all we can."

LISTENING EAR

"Plans fail for lack of counsel, but with many advisors they succeed." (Proverbs 15:22)

- Providing positive feedback as preparation commences and vital decisions have to be made.
- Talking through any anxieties or fears to encourage trust and confidence in God.
- Listening for what God might be saying, or wanting you to say to them. "Giving an encouraging 'word

in season' means you need to know what season it is!" (Mike Frith – *Sender's Guide*)

GENUINE FRIENDSHIPS

- Helping them to keep their eyes on Jesus during periods of delay or disappointment.
- Encouraging them to take one step at a time towards their intended goal.
- Assisting them with preparation by looking out for materials/contacts relevant to their chosen area of future ministry.
- Keeping their feet on the ground by reminding them of the importance of other members/ministries within the Body of Christ.

PRAYER

- Both with them and for them!
- Agreeing together in prayer over specific practical needs and rejoicing together when God answers!

Ensure people in the church and those sent are clear on the whole area of 'expectations'. Often people spend their first few years in a new nation learning the language and adapting to the culture. People can feel pressured, and their morale dented if, in the early years people from home are constantly asking, "How many people have you seen saved?"

LOGISTICAL SUPPORT

This section is about providing resources that enable people to perform their particular cross-cultural ministry in an effective manner. As leaders you will need to agree a number of policy matters as well as addressing the more practical "nuts and bolts" dimensions.

In conjunction with your apostolic team, we would suggest you should give thought to the following areas.

Policy Matters

Accountability

The lines of apostolic and pastoral accountability need to be clear between the person(s) sent, the receiving base (if there is one), yourselves and all other parties involved.

- What are the demarcation lines of responsibility between the various parties?

- How is accountability to be achieved? (For example: reports, visits, phone calls, SKYPE or other real time technologies, etc.)
- How often will this take place?
- Would people be served by some kind of written document setting out the agreed procedures?

Finance

You will need to decide what proportion of the needed funds will be financed by the local church or whether the person themselves should raise some or all of their own finances.

- How long will the church commit itself to financial support?
- How are budgets to be reviewed and finances accounted for?
- How will any payments be made and what provision will you make for emergency funds to be sent?

Pastoral care

Where people are received into a local church in another nation the primary burden of pastoral care for workers will fall on the leadership of that local church. Even so, you will no doubt want to retain some level of prayerful and supportive pastoral interest.

However, when your people are in a pioneer situation and no local church has yet been established, then your level of pastoral support will probably be greater. You therefore need to be clear on the following questions:

- Who will take the main pastoral responsibility for the welfare of your people?
- How will you communicate with your people to assess their spiritual state?
- What plans will you make for regular pastoral visits to them in their country of service?

Contingency

You will also need to think through what you will do if a crisis occurs while people are serving abroad. (For example shortage of finance; illness; death of a relative; overthrow of government; persecution; imprisonment; etc.)

In some cases a Crisis Policy would be advisable. For advice and guidance on developing a Crisis Policy contact your apostolic team.

LOGISTICS

LOGISTICS TEAM

To deal with the more practical side of facilitating their ministry, it is wise to engage a team of helpers. We would suggest that the people you need to involve would be best to have some or all of the following characteristics:

- Both practical and spiritual (see Acts 6)
- Gifts of administration/helps (see 1 Corinthians 12:28)
- Diligent – not a five-minute wonder!
- Persevering – able to overcome set-backs.
- Punctual – responds to requests on time.
- Creative – good at problem solving
- Honest – sound business practice/good record keeping.

- Vigilant – eye for detail/keeps abreast of changes.

There are a number of areas the logistics team could help with both before and after people leave to serve abroad. The following are examples of how the team could help in four key areas:

PERSONAL BELONGINGS

- Sale or storage of household items/belongings.
- Sending belongings from storage on request.
- Sale/lease/rent of property. (N.B. A power of attorney could be issued to allow the team to deal with these issues on your workers behalf.)
- Purchase/sending of new items.
- Care of family pets.

PERSONAL COMMITMENTS

- Completion of official forms (for example tax returns, elections, etc.)
- Care of elderly relatives.
- Care of children that remain in the UK/home nation for education.

PERSONAL FINANCES

- Making regular payments in home country.
- Receipt/transfer of funds to another nation.
- Handling tax advice/returns.
- Paying insurances (For example: building, life, health, etc.)

PERSONAL MINISTRY NEEDS

- Sending needed tools and equipment (For example: books, CDs, computer, etc.)
- Sending specialist items (For example: solar cooker)
- Sending resources to facilitate social action (For example: medical supplies, food, clothing, etc.)

The above are only examples. You may well be able to add to this list by writing down all the things that might need attention if you were going away for two years!

The Oscar website (www.oscar.org.uk) provides help for both sourcing supplies and shipping items to workers overseas.

FINANCE SUPPORT

This is a vital area of support and one that needs to grow if all those currently indicating a call to cross-cultural work are to find their way to the nations.

This is not the place to underscore the biblical teaching on giving and generosity, but we would encourage you to review the subject regularly in the life of your church and ensure that you continue to teach upon it from time to time.

"Being generous is also about the devolution of personal choice, meaning that we limit our lifestyle choices so that others with greater or particular needs might improve theirs." (Mike Frith – *Senders Guide*)

In the previous section we stated that you would have to decide your own policy on the amount of funding made available to your people, both for their personal support and resources for their ministry. However, no matter what level of church support is decided upon you do need to confirm that the person(s) have adequate financial provision for their term of service overseas.

It would be good to complete discussions early on the financial provision of such things as pensions, children's education, and income from property, to confirm that adequate arrangements are being put in place to secure their current and future well-being.

As a general rule of thumb: where people are involved in short-term teams (i.e. up to three months' duration) we would encourage them to find their own funding. Raising one's own finance can be a great faith builder as people see God meeting their needs.

Similarly where short-term is a period of up to two years you can encourage them to raise their own finance or to pay a proportion of the costs alongside the local church. In today's climate of early retirement there are an increasing number of retired people that are now able and willing to finance themselves for short-term work.

Generally in the past, those working long-term received the full financial support of the local church. This is still an option, but increasingly people are making their own contribution to funding alongside the local church. Some are financing themselves completely through working as 'tentmakers' or in some other professional capacity. Each case warrants looking at on its own merits.

Try to ensure the amount you give is included in the church budget and is paid regularly to your overseas worker. Receiving a regular amount helps a worker to have some financial stability and to plan their own expenditure. Remember that 'accountability' does not mean expecting the worker to justify how they have spent every penny they have been given to live on!

Do ensure that any financial church commitment by the church is not 'open ended' and provides for regular review as well as possible termination points. If at any time you decide to decrease someone's support amount, give them plenty of warning.

Consideration must also be given to 'hidden' costs such as regular pastoral visits to workers and their families; bringing folk home to the UK or home nation; travel to key conferences or training; and any costs related to contingency plans.

You must prayerfully come to your own policy decision on financial support, but we would highly recommend that you consider the following questions from time to time by way of a challenge to your local church support of world mission:

- Does your local church budget evidence an increasing proportion being spent on mission both at home and in other nations?
- Are you praying regularly for an increase in people's income so that they can give more away to the work of the kingdom? (See Deuteronomy 8:17-18, Psalm 67:1-2 & 6-7, Luke 6:38)
- Are you exercising faith by giving beyond your ability? (See 2 Corinthians 8:1-7)
- Are you taking the opportunity to put people's natural gifts, skills and abilities to work to generate more funds for the kingdom? (For example: selling arts and crafts, tithing professional services, etc.)
- Are you helping your people to consider the issues that surround living a simpler lifestyle for the sake of the gospel? (For example: Do potential upgrades of existing products or services demonstrate a

proven benefit or are they simply another status symbol?)

- Are you taking full advantage of any monies available in your local area for social action in other nations? (For example: Trust Funds often welcome applications for grants for young people going to other nations in a voluntary capacity. Similarly, the European Union is makes funds available to sponsor cultural exchanges between young people in different parts of Europe.)
- Are you making full use of financial benefits? (For example: Tax refunds through Gift Aid, etc.)
- Is your current financial support of those already working in cross-cultural settings sufficient to meet their daily needs or is there scope for some adjustments?

PRAYER SUPPORT

Prayer has a vital role in mobilizing and supporting the church in world mission. (See Matthew 9:37-38).

Prayer not only gets people to other nations but also sustains them in the work and brings about fresh advances for the kingdom of God. (N.B. Prayer can be dangerous!!! In the eighteenth century the first Moravian congregation in London had 72 members. As they continued to pray for world mission 65 of them went into full-time Christian service!)

CORPORATE PRAYER

Do make a point of praying regularly for your people in corporate gatherings and ensure the church is made aware of specific prayer requests. The key here is to be creative in communicating information that the church needs to act upon.

With modern communication it is possible to keep abreast of the current state of affairs of those serving cross-culturally. Why not draw up a schedule among the leaders (or a small team) detailing when each one will contact those in other nations to ask after their welfare and ascertain specific prayer requests? Don't forget to share answers to prayer both to give thanks to God and to keep the saints persevering in prayer.

Prayer team

Whenever possible supplement corporate prayer by small group(s) who have a particular burden or interest in the ministry of your people serving in another nation. This group could also handle prayer requests that are of a more sensitive nature that you would not wish to publicise in larger public gatherings. They could also be responsible for the production and distribution of prayer information for use by other church members.

Prayer letters/prayer chain

Please remember that it is not appropriate to publicly display prayer letters of those serving in restricted entry nations. Personal distribution and circulation of such prayer letters should be handled with the utmost confidence.

Generally obtaining information from those serving in another nation is not a problem. In fact information overload is much more likely to be the problem!

What is important is that any communication is appropriate, relevant and understandable to those receiving the information. People need to be able to act on the information given. This means the days of simply receiving the information from those in other nations, copying it for everyone or pinning it up on a notice board should be over! (N.B. simply forwarding it to others by email may be quicker but does not necessarily mean the content will be understood!)

Remember that there will be people in the church who can't cope with prayer letters just as they arrive. Some will find reading difficult, except for headlines and a few short sentences. Others are used to getting their information via email or mobile phone.

Someone needs to take the information received and contextualise it for different audiences in the church. The material may need to be reduced or re-written or even passed on in a verbal form, perhaps through a prayer chain over the phone. Headlines could also be flashed up through a short PowerPoint presentation during corporate gatherings.

PRAYER GUIDE

People often do not know how to pray for those working in other nations, and the following headings based on a seven-day cycle may be a good starting point for some:

Day 1 — Relationship with God

Day 2 — Physical and emotional needs

Day 3 — Family relationships

Day 4 — Ability to communicate

Day 5 — Effective ministry

Day 6 — Team relationships

Day 7 — Country of service

(Taken from: *Praying for mission partners* For the full article see Global Connections Resourcing Churches – www.globalconnections.org.uk)

N.B. Don't forget to pray for your business people travelling abroad; while we may not always class them as cross-cultural workers they often have great opportunities to share their faith.

COMMUNICATION SUPPORT

Paul's letters in the New Testament reveal that he did not simply have a working relationship or partnership with the saints of God but that between them there was genuine personal warmth and affection. Their friendship was cemented by good communication between them, and Paul was often disturbed when he had no news of their welfare. (See 2 Corinthians 7:5-7, 1 Thessalonians 2:17-3:5)

We can serve people by ensuring life links are maintained by good two-way communication. We should not only show interest in their spiritual health but also in the everyday affairs of daily living. It would be great if such communication happened naturally but in reality you may need to administer this area by setting up some form of rota or by regularly prompting folk into action!

The suggestions that follow will point you in the right direction towards maintaining genuine friendships with those serving in a cross-cultural context. This is not an extensive list, but hopefully will act as a stimulus to your own creative thinking.

- Regular exchange of news – letters, phone calls, emails, SKYPE, social media, etc. (N.B. Don't forget to send photos and to also get the children involved.)
- Send cards/greetings on birthdays, anniversaries and special occasions.

- Encourage small groups to prepare and send individual family news together either video or audio
- Supply news of current church life. (For example: Sunday bulletin, magazine, video of Christmas party, letters to members, reports of 'family' meetings, prophetic words, profile of new members, etc.)
- Send items to promote spiritual growth (For example: CDs, links to websites, new books, Christian magazines, etc.)
- Provide an update on current affairs; this is information that is unobtainable in their own country. (For example: local/national newspaper, sports magazine, Radio Times, website links)
- Send small 'luxury' items unavailable in their country of service along with a short note of encouragement! (For example: chocolate, jars of Marmite(?!), toiletries, the latest new novel, music CDs)

- Where feasible, encourage contact with people who are visiting the same country on business or holiday.

N.B. In 'restricted access' nations you will need to take advice from your workers as to what is/is not acceptable in their particular situation (For example: newspapers that are critical of the host country, certain religious words/terms, etc.)

RE-ENTRY SUPPORT

The Book of Acts reminds us that not only was Paul sent out from a local church base, but that he also returned to that same base to give a report of how God had blessed his ministry among the Gentiles. No doubt he also took time out for rest and refreshment, and together with the church sought God before being sent out again on the next phase of his apostolic ministry. (See Acts 13:1-3, Acts 14:26-28)

Returning home after living in a different culture for some time can be both a joy and a painful experience. The following suggestions are designed to assist you in making the return of your cross-cultural workers as easy and as beneficial as possible to all parties concerned.

(For a fuller treatment of this particular section please refer to the book *The Re-entry Team* by Neal Pirolo, which is in the recommended reading list.)

PRE-RETURN

- Confirm dates of travel and arrange for a 'welcome party' and/or transport from point of arrival to home base.
- Make arrangements for their living accommodation while staying in the UK (N.B. where relevant, stock the home with groceries, toiletries, flowers, etc.) (Note: If they are returning to their own home, make sure that it is ready for their occupation – clean, tidy, and garden in order – as well as stocking the home with groceries, etc.)
- Decide whether or not you will make a vehicle available for their use either for a period or throughout their home stay.
- Schedule in time for them to meet with the elders for a debriefing session and to discuss how best they can share all their news with the church.

- Arrange dates for them to share with the church family about their ministry. (N.B. Don't forget to include time sharing with the children and young people)

    Note: People returning will need more than one opportunity to share what has happened while they have been serving in another nation. Multiple occasions to share will not only benefit the church family in their understanding of what has taken place, but will also benefit the returning workers by helping them to process both the good and bad aspects of their time abroad.

Arrival

- Assist them in fielding invites for meals/coffee from church members so that they are not overwhelmed by people's hospitality.
- Make opportunities for them to get to know people that have joined the church during their absence.

- Facilitate any health checks that may be necessary or prudent while they are home. (For example: doctor, dentist and optician.)
- Advise them on any relevant changes in society that will impact them while home in the UK. (For example: standards/values, education, fashion, music, TV programmes etc.)
- Help them with the purchase of new items for themselves or their ministry. (For example: they may need to purchase clothes items unavailable in their country of service or simply because fashion has moved on – this is of particular relevance to teenagers!)
- Arrange for one or two special outings or a holiday break while they are home. Alternatively, you may wish to give them a gift to spend as they desire during their stay.

Pastoral care

Remember people returning to the UK will often have a mixture of emotional feelings and reactions as they engage again with their home culture. (For example: joy, elation, depression, disappointment, anger, frustration, failure or guilt)

Both parents and children may feel out of touch and isolated even among long-standing friends. It is not at all unusual for them to feel Christians in their home country are half-hearted in their commitment to Christ and they can often see deficiencies in church life that we have overlooked. If people are with you for an extended period do encourage them to share with you their observations on church life. You may get some surprises, good and bad, but it will prove beneficial to the long-term development of your local church life. It will also endorse to them that you value their contribution!

The important thing is to have a listening ear so that they can work through their feelings and express what is on their hearts. Regular meetings are important to move things beyond the superficial to the heart of many matters. This is not an excuse for off-loading pent-up frustrations, but if handled in a godly manner it will allow real hurts to be healed, genuine understanding to be gained and all parties to be enriched.

At the end of this book you will find an example of a debriefing questionnaire that you might like to use or adapt in order to help you understand your workers 'story' from their time abroad. (N.B. Do remember that you also need to talk with the children, particularly those in their teenage years.)

Neal Pirolo, in his helpful book, points out that there are five re-entry patterns regularly found among those returning home. Those seeking to give good pastoral care should be aware of each of these five patterns. The first four should give cause for concern, whereas the fifth is the pattern one would like to see with all returning workers!

ALIENATION

- Feeling negative about his/her home culture.
- Begins to withdraw – making excuses not to see people.
- Feels there is no one to talk to; no one who could possibly understand; no one to help process his/her thoughts.

CONDEMNATION

- Feeling negative about his/her home culture.

- Begins to evidence a judgmental and critical attitude (For example: "People are so uncaring"; "There is such a lack of zeal"; etc.)

REVERSION

- Denies things have moved on! (i.e. that he/she has changed, church has changed, culture has changed.)
- Keeps trying to fit into what was, but no longer is!
- Accepts readily any task put before him/her without thinking about it!

THE ULTIMATE ESCAPE

- Result of the gradual deterioration of any one of the three above.
- Begins to back out of life – spiritually, mentally and emotionally.
- Can lead to suicidal feelings or actual suicide.

INTEGRATION

- Adjusts and settles back comfortably into the home environment.

This last pattern is more likely to be seen when people:

- Have been supported well during their preparation time and during their service in another nation.
- Model re-entry on a biblical pattern (For example: Paul in Acts 14:26-28, Acts 15:35)
- Are sure their home-coming is at the Holy Spirit's direction.
- Return to their sending church where they are known.
- Receive the hospitality and care of genuine friends.
- Are able to share ALL that has happened to them.
- Become active again in ministry at home.

Pirolo also states there are nine areas that can cause stress to the returning worker:

PHYSICAL

- 'Jet lag', changes in climate, diet, pace of life, on-going health issues

Professional

- Loss of job skills, need to earn a living again, work practices, etc.

Financial

- Money being short, jealousy of others that 'have', austerity versus hedonism!

Cultural

- Clash of values and attitudes

Social

- Identity and status, friends having moved on

Linguistic

- New words and jargon to be learned; feels inadequate to express himself/herself in mother tongue

National/political

- Have been on the end of 'foreign policy', new government in power/new laws enacted, different perspective on life issues

Educational

- Different standards and values

Spiritual

- Lower level of spirituality? (For example: Home church seemingly majoring on minor-issues while souls perish! Feeling church is apathetic, complacent, or disinterested in issues beyond the local area.)

Stress in any one of these areas needs to be met with a listening ear, understanding and above all wisdom.

Remember that as with bereavement some issues may remain or surface weeks or months after return. It may be necessary therefore to keep a pastoral eye out for your returnees beyond the initial days and weeks after they return.

Review

This is a good time to examine together the effectiveness of their ministry and to prayerfully seek God for any necessary adjustments. As you seek the Holy Spirit's guidance it should be possible to confirm together the next step for your workers in the purpose of God for their lives.

Some suggested areas for discussion:

- State of the family (i.e. physical, emotional, spiritual)
- Adequacy of financial support
- Children's educational needs
- Relationship with fellow workers
- How to improve support from home base
- Goals/objectives for next period of service
- Training/equipping needed to meet goals
- Tools/equipment/personnel needed for future ministry

7
MAINTAINING THE MOMENTUM

The raising up of new cross-cultural workers and the on-going support of those already engaged in cross-cultural ministry should be the active concern of the whole church, not just of the church leaders and a few world mission enthusiasts or friends of those serving in another culture.

It is a leadership responsibility not only to ensure time and resources are given to this area of church life, but that the church cultivates a supportive climate for cross-cultural workers. Support will die or become ineffective if your people do not live in an atmosphere of world mission.

While there are many legitimate calls on leadership time and we want to be zealous in building vibrant local churches in our communities we should not forget our prophetic call to the nations:

"It is too small a thing for you to be my servant to restore the tribes of Jacob and to bring back those of Israel I have kept. I will also make you a light for the Gentiles; that you may bring my salvation to the ends of the earth." (Isaiah 49:6)

So, how can we as leaders keep the priority of making disciples of all nations before our people? Here are a few suggestions to get you started.

MAINTAIN AN ATMOSPHERE OF WORLD MISSION

- Ensure your congregational teaching centres regularly on God's 'big story' and His purposes for all nations.
- Be intentional in receiving apostolic and prophetic input into your church to inspire and impart faith for reaching the nations. Apostolic ministry equips us to be a 'sent' people, brings news of God's advancing kingdom worldwide, and catches us up in church planting across the nations.

- Look for opportunities to invite people from other ethnic backgrounds to preach/teach in your church. People from your own congregation, outside visitors or guests from overseas.
- Host visitors from overseas (of all ages), especially Christians visiting the UK to attend Christian conferences. Showing hospitality to overseas students and people visiting for business is also another way to increase your people's understanding of our global world.
- Make mention of things happening on the world stage or in current news, and where appropriate pray for these things in public gatherings.
- Refer regularly to past and present examples of those who have given or are giving their lives to extend God's kingdom around the world. You may want to recommend inspiring biographies of such people or point them to articles about their lives on the Internet.

- Obtain up to date information on the persecuted church around the world and pray regularly for brothers and sisters in those situations.

Maintain the focus on the cross-cultural worker(s)

- Commission people publicly, accompanied by prayer and prophecy.
- Receive people back well, celebrating their time away and the value of what has been accomplished.
- Provide multiple church settings where your worker can share the story of their time away.
- Regularly provide the church with up to date news of your worker that is appropriate, relevant and understandable.
- With modern technologies you might like to try a live link-up during one of your Sunday or mid-week gatherings.
- Profile your overseas workers on any new member's course that you run. (N.B. Why not send your workers photos of new members!)

- Highlight stories in the news that come from the country where your people are working and where appropriate pray about the situation.

8
DEBRIEFING QUESTIONNAIRE

The following outline is given to help you discover the 'story' of your worker and provide them with an opportunity to bring 'closure' on an important period of their life. The questions are a guide/framework for you to use in order to encourage your worker to speak openly about their experience. (It is not intended that every question should be asked or that the time would degenerate into a minor interrogation session!)

Do be sensitive to both the Holy Spirit's leading and the dignity of your worker. Don't be intrusive or probe unnecessarily but allow your worker to share their story in their own time and in their own way. In many instances it will be necessary to meet with your worker a number of times in order for them to reveal their true feelings about their experiences both good and bad.

Most 'issues' that arise from this session will be able to be handled within the normal framework of your pastoral care system. However, on some occasions you may need to obtain specialist help in order to resolve the issue. (For example: specialist counselling, medical/psychiatric help)

INTRODUCTION

The purpose of this debriefing:

- Reflect on your experience
- Say whatever you like!

OVERVIEW

- Can you give us an overview of your time in the nation?
- Describe your experiences (in brief) – good & bad.
- What is the most significant lesson you learned?
- How did you get on with your team, church members and the locals?

- Any specific things you would like to talk about?

TROUBLING OR STRESSFUL EXPERIENCES

- As you look back on the whole experience, what was the worst, most stressful or troubling experience for you?
- Describe any specific events, or stressful parts of the experience.
- Can you pick out the three most important ones as far as you are concerned?

UNPACKING THE SPECIFICS

For each of the three you have chosen:

- Can you share the details of the issue/event?
- Say what you thought about the issue/event then and what you think about it now.
- Describe how you felt when it was happening and how you feel now.

ANY OTHER MATTER

Is there any other matter or concern you would like to voice concerning your period of service in the nation? For example:

- Administrative problems?
- Support from home base?
- Unmet expectations?
- Family difficulties?

STRESS-RELATED SYMPTOMS

Have you experienced any of the following symptoms at any point either while in the nation or since returning home?

- Tiredness, sleeping problems, nightmares
- Appetite changes, nausea
- Irritability, depressed mood, concentration or memory difficulties
- Flashbacks or repeatedly thinking about what happened
- Trying to avoid thinking about your time in the nation
- Sense of anger, guilt or meaninglessness

- Change in your view of the world
- Inability to relax
- Difficulty in making decisions
- Tearful or unable to cry

RECOVERY AND SUPPORT

The above symptoms are normal!

What are you doing to reduce your stress levels?

- Allowing sufficient time to rest?
- Engaging in physical exercise?
- Doing things you find relaxing or enjoyable?
- Spending time with your family?
- Who are you talking to now?
- Who will you talk to in the future?

POSITIVE ASPECTS OF THE TRIP

- What were the best aspects of your time in the nation?
- What did you learn?

- Do you feel you helped people and made a difference?
- Were friendships/relationships formed or deepened?
- Did you achieve some or all of your goals?
- Any helpful insights or recommendations for the future?

RETURNING HOME

- What have you found most difficult since returning home?
- Do you have any current worries?
- Are you experiencing any relationship difficulties?

THE FUTURE

- What plans do you have for the immediate future?
- Any changes to your long-term plans?
- What are your goals and objectives for the next period?

- Do you need any training or more resources for the next stage?

Do you have any questions or anything else you would like to say?

9
RECOMMENDED READING

There is a wealth of resources that can help in preparation for cross-cultural mission. Here are just some of the ones I recommend and use:

THEOLOGY / MISSIOLOGY

Missionary Methods – St. Paul's or ours? Roland Allen (Eerdmans)
An examination of St. Paul's own principles for missionary work

Jesus through Middle Eastern Eyes, Kenneth E. Bailey (SPCK)
Cultural studies in the gospels

Paul through Mediterranean Eyes, Kenneth E. Bailey (SPCK)
Cultural studies in 1 Corinthians

Poet & Peasant and Through Peasant Eyes, Kenneth E. Bailey (Eerdmans)
Cultural framework and literary structure of the parables in the gospel of Luke

The Gospel to the Nations, ed. Peter Bolt & Mark Thompson (Apollos)
Perspectives on Paul's Mission

Transforming Mission, D. Bosch (Orbis Books)
Paradigm shifts in the theology of mission

What On Earth Is The Church For? David Devenish (Authentic Media)
A radical approach to church mission and social action

Fathering Leaders, Motivating Mission, David Devenish (Authentic Media)
Restoring the role of the apostle in today's church

A Time for Mission, S. Escobar (IVP)
The challenge for global Christianity

Kingdom Concerns, K. Gnanakan (IVP)
A re-examination of mission in the light of a biblical emphasis upon the kingdom of God resolving the relationship between evangelism and social action

Proclaiming Christ in a Pluralistic Context, Ken Gnanakan (Theological Book Trust)
The challenge - exclusivism, inclusivism and pluralism

Good News for All Nations, M. Goldsmith (Hodder & Stoughton)
Mission at the heart of the New Testament

Mapping Messianic Jewish Theology, Richard Harvey (Paternoster)
A study of the diverse theological terrain of this young movement

God of the Poor, D. Hughes and M. Bennett (OM Publishing)
A biblical vision of God's present rule

Territorial Spirits and World Evangelisation, Chuck Lowe (OMF International)

Exploring a more biblically legitimate and effective model in spiritual warfare

The Open Secret, Lesslie Newbigin (Eerdmans/ SPCK)
An introduction to the theology of mission

The Gospel in a Pluralist Society, Lesslie Newbigin (SPCK)
Analysis of contemporary culture and how Christians can confidently affirm their faith

Biblical Christianity in African Perspective, Wilbur O'Donovan (Paternoster Press)
Survey of the major truths of the Christian faith as seen from the perspective of the traditional African worldview

The Twilight Labyrinth, George Otis Jr. (Chosen Books)
Why does spiritual darkness linger where it does?

The Message of Mission, H. Peskett and V. Ramachandra (IVP)
This East-West partnership in missiological exploration expounds a variety of Old and New Testament texts and examines a wide range of issues

Let the Nations Be Glad, John Piper (IVP)
Making God supreme in missions

Against The Stream, D. W. Smith (IVP)
Christianity and mission in an age of globalization

Seeking a City With Foundations, David W, Smith (IVP)
Theology for an urban world

One World or Many? ed. Richard Tiplady (William Carey Library)
The impact of globalisation on mission

Postmission ed. Richard Tiplady (Paternoster Press)
World Mission by a postmodern generation

Salvation Belongs To Our God, Chris Wright (IVP)
Celebrating the Bible's central story

The Mission of God, Christopher J. H. Wright (IVP)
Unlocking the Bible's grand narrative

MOTIVATING THE LOCAL CHURCH

Iran – Open Hearts in a Closed Land, Mark Bradley (Authentic Media)
Accurate and up-to-date picture of the present day situation

Hidden Sorrow Lasting Joy, Anneke Companjen (Hodder & Stoughton)
The forgotten women of the persecuted church

Why Bother With Mission? S. Gaukroger (IVP)
An introduction to understanding and becoming involved in mission

Global Passion, David Greenlee (Authentic Lifestyle)
Lessons from the life of George Verwer (Founder of Operation Mobilisation)

Crossing the Divide, Owen Hylton (IVP)
Crossing the divide and embracing diversity as God's plan and purpose for his church

Connect! T. Jeffery & S. Chalke (Spring Harvest)
Launching the twenty-first century Church into a new paradigm of mission

Churches Going Global – Connect! 2, T. Jeffery and R. Johnson (Spring Harvest)
14 stories of churches with a global mission

Operation World (21st Century Edition), P. Johnstone & J. Mandryk (WEC International)
An alphabetical and regional listing for every country of the world, with general information and specific points for prayer

The Church Is Bigger Than You Think, P. Johnstone (Christian Focus)
Provides a framework to understand what God is doing in our world, why He is doing it and how we can be part of the action

Where There Was No Church, ed E J Martin (Learning Together Press)
Postcards from followers of Jesus in the Muslim World

RECOMMENDED READING

Loving the Church – Blessing the Nations, George Miley (Gabriel Publishing)
Pursuing the role of local churches in Global Mission

Dynamic Diversity, Bruce Milne (IVP)
The new humanity church for today and tomorrow

Real-time Connections, Bob Roberts Jr (Zondervan)
Linking your job with God's global work

Window on the World, Daphne Spraggett & Jill Johnstone (Paternoster)
When we pray God works

Catch the Vision 2000, B & A Stearns (Bethany House)
Shows a multitude of practical ways for individuals and churches to become involved in God's mission to reach the nations

Forbidden Faith, ed. Mervyn Thomas (CWR)
Devotions and stories from the persecuted church around the world

Out of the Comfort Zone, George Verwer (OM Publishing)
For servant leaders who want to understand better what God is doing and wanting to do across the world

PASTORAL CARE

Ad-mission, G. Fawcett (YWAM)
The briefing and debriefing of teams of missionaries and aid workers

Honourably Wounded, M. F. Foyle (MARC)
Stress among Christian workers.

Love across Latitudes, Janet Fraser-Smith (Pioneers International)
A workbook on cross-cultural marriage

The Call, Os Guinness (Paternoster)
Finding and fulfilling the central purpose of your life

Doing Member Care Well, ed. K. O'Donnell (William Carey Library)
Perspectives and practices from around the world.

Serving as Senders, N. Pirolo (Emmaus Road)
Six ways to care for missionaries – while they are preparing to go; while they are on the field; when they return home

The Re-Entry Team, N. Pirolo (Emmaus Road)
Discovering the problem and the solution

Intercultural Marriage, Dugan Romano (Nicholas Brealey Publishing)
Promises and Pitfalls

Too Valuable To Lose, ed. W.D Taylor (William Carey Library)
Exploring the causes and cures of missionary attrition

WORKERS GOING OVERSEAS

Friend Raising, B. Barnett (YWAM)
Building a missionary support team that lasts

Demolishing Strongholds, David Devenish (Word Publishing)
Effective strategies for spiritual warfare

Nothing Else To Fear, D. W. Ellis (OMF)
Holding fast to God in tough times

Servant Ministry, Tony Horsfall (BRF)
A portrait of Christ and a pattern for his followers

Re-Entry, R Jordan (YWAM)
Making the transition from missions to life at home – practical guide

Families on the Move, M. Knell (Monarch)
Growing up overseas and loving it! A practical guide

Burn-up or Splash Down, M. Knell (Authentic)
The re-entry experience and adapting to life back home

The Travellers' Good Health Guide, T. Lankester (Sheldon Press)
All you need to know to stay healthy abroad.

The World Christian, R. Thompson (St John's Extension Studies)
A workbook for those aiming to take the gospel from culture to culture

Entering Another's World, M. Wardell & R. Thompson (St John's Extension Studies)

A workbook for those who want to learn how to live for God in another culture

My Rights, My God, R. Wells (Monarch)
Facing the implications of God's call to serve in another culture

Funding the Family Business, Myles Wilson (Stewardship)
A handbook for raising personal support

SPECIFIC CROSS-CULTURAL ISSUES

Embracing the Poor, ed. David Adams (Roper Penberthy)
Releasing, resourcing and equipping the poor for world mission

Strange Virtues, B T. Adeney (IVP)
Ethics across cultures – exploring how the Bible and culture interact to produce ethical stances (Particular case studies)

Daughters of Islam, Miriam Adeney (IVP)
Building bridges with Muslim women

No God But God, Reza Aslan (Arrow Books)
The origins, evolution and future of Islam

Gospel for Muslims, Steve Bell (Authentic Media)
Learning to read the Bible through eastern eyes

Grace for Muslims, Steve Bell (Authentic Media)
Moving from prejudice to understanding and from fear to friendship

Friendship First (the manual), Steve Bell (Friendship First)
Ordinary Christians discussing good news with ordinary Muslims

Between Naivety and Hostility, ed. Steve Bell & Colin Chapman (Authentic Media)
Uncovering the best Christian responses to Islam in Britain

Clash of Worlds, D. Burnett (MARC)
The major contemporary worldviews and basic principles of evangelizing those with other perspectives

Reaching Muslims, Nick Chatrath (Monarch)
A one-stop guide for Christians

Cross and Crescent, Colin Chapman (IVP)
A guide to Islamic beliefs and practices

Global Mission, ed. Rose Dowsett (William Carey Library)
Reflections and case studies in contextualisation for the whole church

When Helping Hurts, Steve Corbett & Brian Fikkert (Moody Publishers)
How to alleviate poverty without hurting the poor

Communicating Christ Cross-Culturally (2nd Edition), D. J. Hesselgrave (Zondervan)
Communication and mission; communication and culture

Planting Churches Cross-Culturally, D. J. Hesselgrave (Baker Book House)
A guide for home and foreign missions

God's New Tribe, John Kpikpi (Hill City Publishing)
God's answer to tribalism and racism

Mentoring For Mission, Gunter Krallman (Jensco)
A handbook on leadership principles exemplified by Jesus Christ

Ministering Cross-Culturally, S. G. Lingenfelter and M. K. Mayers (Baker Book House, Grand Rapids ISBN: 0-8010-5632-2)
God's model for human relationships

The World's Religions (Lion Publishing)
Comprehensive guide to the world's religions, past and present, designed for non-specialists

Emerging Hope, Jimmy Long (IVP)
A strategy for reaching postmodern generations

Muslims, Magic and the Kingdom of God, Rick Love (William Carey Library)
A guide to church planting among Muslims

Miniskirts, Mothers and Muslims, Christine A. Mallouhi (Monarch)
Conventions that govern Muslim society and the unwitting mistakes Westerners can make

Going Global, Michael Moynagh & Richard Worsley (A & C Black)
Globalisation – Key questions for the 21st Century

RECOMMENDED READING

Touching the Soul of Islam, Bill Musk, (Monarch)
Sharing the gospel in Muslim cultures

The Unseen Face of Islam, Bill Musk (Monarch)
Understanding folk-Islam and sharing the gospel with ordinary Muslims

Faith and Power, Lesslie Newbigin, Lamin Sanneh & Jenny Taylor (Wipf & Stock)
Christianity and Islam in "Secular" Britain

The Poor Deserve the Best, Nigel Ring (Newfrontiers)
A manual for good practice for working with the poor

A Vison of the Possible, Daniel Sinclair (Authentic)
Pioneer church planting in teams

A Christian's Pocket Guide to Islam, Patrick Sookhdeo (Christian Focus)
Factual information and practical advice

Distinctly Welcoming, Richard Sudworth (Scripture Union)
Christian presence in a multi-faith society

The Koran for Dummies, Sohaib Sultan (Wiley Publishing)
History, structure and basic tenets of Islam's sacred scripture

From Seed to Fruit, ed. J. Dudley Woodberry (William Carey Library)
Global trends, fruitful practices, and emerging issues among Muslims

THE WORLD CHRISTIAN MOVEMENT

World Mission: An Analysis of the World Christian Movement Vol 1,2 & 3 (2nd Edition), ed J. Lewis (William Carey Library)
God's purpose and plan, strategy for world evangelisation, mission and culture

Perspectives on the World Christian Movement A Reader (Revised Edition) ed. R. Winter & S. Hawthorne (William Carey Library)
Addresses the Biblical, Historical, Cultural and Strategic perspectives on missions

10
QUESTIONNAIRES

The following questionnaires are based on the material presented in the earlier part of this book. (N.B. They were adapted from questionnaires regularly used in preparing people for cross-cultural mission by the leadership team at Dartford Christian Fellowship, and are based on the first edition of this book from 1997.)

These questionnaires are designed for people to complete before meeting up with their church leadership team and provide a basis for open discussion about the possibilities of involvement in cross-cultural mission in other nations.

Alternatively, leadership teams may like to select specific questions from this series of questionnaires in order to form their own list of discussion topics for open dialogue with their people.

Depending on the leadership team's knowledge of individual people and situations, it may only be necessary to ask people to complete one or two questionnaires rather than the complete set.

The questionnaires cover the following topics:

1. Character and personality profile 1
2. Character and personality profile 2
3. Relational skills
4. Emotional & physical health; qualifications/work experience; skills
5. Family matters – singles, married and parents
6. Motivation & realism
7. Spiritual life and ministry
8. Call of God
9. Children and Young People's Questionnaire – How they feel about going abroad.

QUESTIONNAIRE 1

We would like you to complete this questionnaire as honestly as you can. It will be treated confidentially and used as a basis for further discussion with you about the way forward.

1. How would you describe your Christian life over the last 12 months? (For example: up and down, steady, exciting, consistent)

2. In what ways do you feel you have grown and matured in the last year?

3. What areas of weakness and temptation do you struggle with the most?

4. How would other people in the church, outside of your close friends, describe you?

5. If we were to ask your current employer for a character reference, what would you expect him/her to say?

6. What type of work do you love to do and what kind of work do you hate?

7. Have you ever been dismissed from employment? If "Yes", what was the reason?

8. How would you rate your ability to manage your own (and/or your family's) finances?

9. Have you any outstanding debts? If "Yes", how are you planning to clear them?

10. What sort of things make you feel pressurised, stressed or frustrated?

11. Which of the following would you most tend towards?
    a. Lack of self-control   b. Lack of self-discipline
    c. Perfectionism   d. Being a workaholic

12. How do you balance your time between work, family, church and leisure?

13. What do you do to relax?

14. Who are your six closest friends?

15. What sort of things would you regard as personal failure?

N.B. If someone else were to read your answers to these questions without knowing who wrote them, would they recognise you?

QUESTIONNAIRE 2

We would like you to complete this questionnaire as honestly as you can. It will be treated confidentially and used as a basis for further discussion with you about the way forward.

1. What learning setting is best suited to your own spiritual development? (For example: Sunday morning, cell group, private study, conferences, 'in life')

2. What has God been teaching you over the last two months?

3. Can you give any examples of the ways in which God has taught you things through people or situations that you would not have expected?

4. Outline any particular areas where you have found that your views have completely changed through the teaching you have received.

5. Describe one incident where you feel you were good at taking correction and another where you found it very difficult?

6. How do you react if you are criticised or wronged personally? (For example: do you defend or justify yourself, forgive, struggle with your emotions, …?)

7. Galatians 5:22-23 lists the fruit of the Spirit. Order your perception of this fruit in your life by allocating a score of 1 through to 9 to each particular facet (1 being where you are strongest and 9 where you are weakest)

   Love ( )   Patience ( )   Faithfulness ( )
   Joy ( )   Kindness ( )   Gentleness ( )
   Peace ( )   Goodness ( )   Self-control ( )

8. Could people describe you as a person who does 'good works' and if so to what do you think they would be referring?

9. How would you show generosity to others if you were living on a limited budget?

10. Would you say that you are the type of person who would:
    - Volunteer for anything?
    - Volunteer for anything that you considered your gifting?
    - Volunteer if nobody else seemed to offer?
    - Volunteer to do things even when there is no direct request for help?

11. What areas in your life would you say you are very particular about? (For example: cleanliness, clothes and appearance, possessions)

12. List some things you do for sheer pleasure or enjoyment.

13. How would you rate your common sense on a scale of 1-10? (1 = 'scatty'; 10 = full of common sense)

14. How would you describe yourself?
    - Someone who finds change difficult and doesn't like it
    - Someone who finds change difficult but accepts it without complaining
    - Someone who is flexible and doesn't mind change
    - Someone who actually enjoys change and gets bored if things don't change regularly

15. Does the unknown excite, challenge or frighten you? Can you explain why?

16. Can you describe any experiences you have had to date that you would classify as adventurous?

17. Would you describe yourself as a person who is able to take personal initiative in most situations or are you more comfortable with receiving and carrying out the instructions of others?

QUESTIONNAIRE 3

We would like you to complete this questionnaire as honestly as you can. It will be treated confidentially and used as a basis for further discussion with you about the way forward.

1. What kinds of people do you find it easier to relate to and work with? (For example: same sex/opposite sex, children, senior citizens, married/singles, etc)

2. Why do you think you find it easier to relate to and work with these kinds of people rather than to others?

3. How do you cope with relating to sick or disabled people?

4. How do you feel you relate to people in the wider body of Christ (i.e. outside your own local church) who hold very different views to yourself?

5. How do you cope with being submissive to those 'over you in the Lord' when you find you disagree with something they have said?

6. What team situations are you involved in?

7. How do you respond when you are given direction/correction and held accountable within a team setting?

8. Give some examples of where you have successfully worked alongside people who are very different to you both in terms of their personality and/or social background.

9. What would your approach be in resolving personal conflict with others?

10. To what extent would you get involved as a 'peacemaker' if it were other people in conflict?

11. If you forgave someone who had wronged you, how willing would you be to work with them/trust them again?

12. Can you give some evidence of your personal interest in other cultures? (For example: friendships, visits, reading, study, prayer, etc.)

13. Describe briefly one cross-cultural encounter or experience that has changed the way you view people from other cultures.

QUESTIONNAIRE 4

We would like you to complete this questionnaire as honestly as you can. It will be treated confidentially and used as a basis for further discussion with you about the way forward.

1. How easy do you find it to give and receive affection?

2. Which of the following best describes your stance towards others?
    - Always on the lookout for something to encourage in them.
    - Will encourage them if they do something particularly well.
    - Ready to empathise with them if they are going through a hard time.

- Easily become impatient or irritated with those who appear constantly downhearted

3. How easy do you find it to make new friends?

4. What do you consider the effect will be on your existing friendships of serving God in another nation?

5. Do you have any on-going commitments or responsibilities towards any family members, and if so, how do you see these being worked out in the future? (For example: elderly parents, brothers/sisters, dependent children etc.)

6. How would you describe your general health?

7. Have you in the past undergone any treatment and/or counselling for any physical, emotional or mental illness?

8. Does any member of your family suffer from any physical/mental illness or handicaps?

9. Have you ever had to leave a job because you felt unable to cope with the stress of it?

10. Do you know of any traumatic past experience that still affects you today?

11. List both your current academic or professional qualifications and any other recognised qualification for which you are currently studying.

12. How would you rate both your ability to learn new skills, and your willingness to re-train in order to obtain a qualification that would gain you entry to another country?

13. What theological training (formal or informal) or other specialist training have you had which you consider would be relevant to building the church in a cross-cultural situation?

14. If your service to the body of Christ has taken place in a number of local churches detail a brief history of how you served in each local church.

15. Try and rate yourself in the following skills areas adding any comments as appropriate.

- Life skills (For example: cooking, hygiene, budgeting etc.)
- DIY skills (For example: painting, decorating, plumbing, carpentry etc.)
- Engineering/mechanical skills (For example: electrics, car maintenance, etc.)
- Medical skills (For example: nursing, first aid, etc.)
- IT skills
- Other skills

16. List your proficiency in any foreign language you speak and rate yourself as to whether or not you enjoy language learning?

QUESTIONNAIRE 5

We would like you to complete this questionnaire as honestly as you can. It will be treated confidentially and used as a basis for further discussion with you about the way forward.

FOR SINGLES

1. What are your current thoughts about the possibility of marriage or remaining single?

2. Do you have any very close friendships or romantic attachments at the moment?

3. If your current thinking is to marry before you go to another nation, how long do you think you should wait after marriage before going to serve cross-culturally?

4. What are your thoughts regarding the possibility of marrying someone from a different culture?

5. What do your parents think about your plans to go to another nation?

FOR MARRIEDS

1. Do you and your partner both have the same vision for cross-cultural work, or does one of you feel more strongly about it than the other?

2. What are the key issues that regularly cause tension in your marriage?

3. Would you say that you and your partner communicate well with each other?

4. What has been your experience of coping with difficulty together since you have been married?

5. Whether or not you currently have children, have you thought through the implications of having and rearing children in a different culture?

FOR PARENTS

1. How do you think your children would cope with living in another nation?

2. If your children are of secondary school age, what does each one think about the idea?

3. What thoughts do you have regarding their education while they are in another nation?

QUESTIONNAIRE 6

We would like you to complete this questionnaire as honestly as you can. It will be treated confidentially and used as a basis for further discussion with you about the way forward.

1. In a few words try and describe what motivates you to want to become involved in cross-cultural ministry.

2. What are the key factors at this present time that make you feel valued as a person?

3. List anything in your current home, work or church situation that you are unhappy about and would like to get away from.

4. What do you think will help you find fulfilment once you are working in a cross-cultural situation?

5. Jesus taught that we need to 'count the cost' of following him (Luke 14:25-35). Which of the following do you consider will be the most costly for yourself and why?
   - The sense of loneliness and separation from family and friends.
   - The difficulties of everyday living.
   - The sacrifice of future career prospects.
   - The difficulties in learning a new language.
   - The reduction in economic status.
   - The possible health risks.

6. What evidence could you offer to show that you know enough about the culture of the people and any potential area of service to make a sound judgement about getting involved?

7. Have you met and/or spoken with anyone who is doing or has done the same kind of work you want to engage in, either in the same cross-cultural setting or one that is very similar?

8. What have been the results of your investigation into the language requirements for your potential cross-cultural assignment?

QUESTIONNAIRE 7

We would like you to complete this questionnaire as honestly as you can. It will be treated confidentially and used as a basis for further discussion with you about the way forward.

1. What words would you use to describe your personal relationship with God?

2. What place do worship and prayer have in your daily life?

3. Can you give one or two examples of the way in which your reading and study of the Bible has strengthened your walk with God?

4. In what ways are you able to recognise the power and presence of the Holy Spirit in your life?

5. Can you give any examples of how your life is affected more by grace than legalism?

6. Give one or two examples of how you personally express your love for the Body of Christ.

7. In what ways would you say your faith has been tested, and how did you stand up under these tests?

8. In what ways do you feel you express your love and concern for the lost?

9. Can you give an example of when your own openness to God has resulted in your carefully made plans being changed?

10. What areas of ministry are you involved in at the moment and what measurable fruit is there of your ministry?

11. What experience have you had in the past in leading, managing, training or discipling others?

12. How do you rate your ability to both hear and understand others and to communicate clearly to them your own thoughts and intentions?

13. What things are you doing now, that you feel may be preparing you for ministry in a different culture?

14. What further training do you think you would benefit from before you go?

15. Is there any training you would expect to receive upon arrival in to your new sphere of service?

QUESTIONNAIRE 8

We would like you to complete this questionnaire as honestly as you can. It will be treated confidentially and used as a basis for further discussion with you about the way forward.

1. Describe in general terms how you have become convinced of God's call on your life to serve Him cross-culturally?

2. Try and summarise any specific prophetic words you have had about this call.

3. Detail any specific guidance you may have received by way of supernatural revelation from the Lord. (For example: visions, dreams, angelic visitations etc)

4. List any scriptures you feel God has used to confirm your call.

5. Can you describe any set of circumstances that you consider have confirmed your call to serve cross-culturally?

6. Do your immediate family members share your conviction about your call, and have their own personal sense of calling?

7. What do your close friends and extended family think about your desire to serve in a cross-cultural situation?

8. What reasons do you have for thinking the church will endorse/not endorse your call and be supportive of you in the future?

QUESTIONNAIRE 9 FOR CHILDREN AND YOUNG PEOPLE

1. What do you think about the idea of moving away to live in another country?

2. Have you shared these thoughts with your parents?

3. Do you understand why your parents want to go?

4. Do you have any friends from another country?

5. Have you learned any other language(s) at school?

6. How does the idea of going abroad to live make you feel? (For example: happy, sad, excited, frightened etc.)

7. What do you think you would miss most about this country?

8. Which particular friends would you really miss loads?

9. Are there any ways in which you think you could keep in touch with your friends in this country?

10. How do you think you will cope without English TV?

11. What do you think it is like where you may be going?

12. Are there any things you are really worried about when you think of living in another country?

13. What do you think are the good and not so good things about going to school in another country?

14. Do you have any questions you would like answered about going abroad?

15. Do you feel ready to go yet or would you rather wait until you are older?

16. How do you think God can help you to prepare to go abroad and then to settle in when you arrive?

TEN OBSERVATIONS ON SHORT-TERM, LONG-TERM AND SECULAR WORK

	SHORT-TERM	**LONG-TERM INVESTMENT**	**SECULAR WORK**
CALL	Opportunity to test	Must be certain	Must be certain (often providential)
COUNTRY	Unrestricted access in most nations	Barred from entering some nations	Particularly good for 'restricted' nations

OBSERVATIONS ON SHORT-TERM, LONG-TERM & SECULAR WORK

	SHORT-TERM	**LONG-TERM INVESTMENT**	**SECULAR WORK**
LANGUAGE	Little or no language	Essential	Level varies (not always 'skilled')
LOGISTICS	Simple (little luggage/ belongings)	Complex (removal, storage, transport, etc.)	Level varies (depends on employers policy)
FINANCE	Relatively cheap (N.B. Can syphon off funds from long-term)	Long-term investment (N.B. Liable to increase with the years)	Self-supporting (N.B. Generous salary can help support emerging work)

	SHORT-TERM	**LONG-TERM INVESTMENT**	**SECULAR WORK**
FAMILY	Remain at home	Must accompany (raises question of children's welfare and education)	Varies according to term of service
CULTURE	Immature/inexperienced response	Integrate/relevant	Danger of isolation (For example: expatriate-ghetto/church)
FRIENDSHIP	Superficial (little time to build)	Strong (build quality relationships but often "religious motives" questioned)	Social penetration (often reach social grouping restricted to others)

OBSERVATIONS ON SHORT-TERM, LONG-TERM & SECULAR WORK

	SHORT-TERM	**LONG-TERM INVESTMENT**	**SECULAR WORK**
LOCAL CHURCH	Generates interest in mission	Requires on-going support	Moral & prayer support needed
OUTCOME	Awareness of need Return as long-termers Mission involvement (N.B. can distract long-termers in their work)	Build national church Integration with culture Meeting real needs Reproducing after 'own' kind	Effective daily witness Respect for secular contribution Extension of kingdom (N.B. often limited in time given to building the church)

www.ingramcontent.com/pod-product-compliance
Lightning Source LLC
Chambersburg PA
CBHW050538300426
44113CB00012B/2158